THE GOSPEL OF THE KINGDOM

THE GOSPEL
OF THE KINGDOM

*Scriptural Studies in
the Kingdom of God*

George Eldon Ladd

William B. Eerdmans Publishing Company
Grand Rapids, Michigan / Cambridge, U.K.

Published by Wm. B. Eerdmans Publishing Co.
2140 Oak Industrial Drive N.E., Grand Rapids, Michigan 49505 /
P.O. Box 163, Cambridge CB3 9PU U.K.

Printed in the United States of America

12 11   33 32

ISBN 978-0-8028-1280-3

www.eerdmans.com

FOREWORD

SERIOUS students of the Bible sometimes lose sight of the fact that the study and interpretation of Scripture should never be an end in itself. God has given men His Word written for a practical purpose: "That the man of God may be complete, equipped for every good work" (II Tim. 3: 17). When a gulf exists between the lecture-room and the pulpit, sterility in the class-room and superficiality in the pulpit often result.

The present author has given much attention to the technical study of the Biblical doctrine of the Kingdom of God. No teaching of the New Testament has been more vigorously debated than this. However, the Kingdom of God was the central message of our Lord's ministry. He "went about all Galilee . . . preaching the gospel of the kingdom" (Matt. 4: 23). This element of proclamation has often been engulfed in debate and argument.

The following pages are proclamation. While it is obvious that a distinct point of view underlies the proclamation, the purpose is not to defend the point of view or to discuss optional interpretations or critical and theological problems, but to attempt to follow our Lord's example by proclaiming Good News.

These studies were originally delivered as addresses in the pulpit and in Bible Conferences and have been recorded and adapted for publication. The style therefore is simple and direct, the objective is devotional and practical, and the appeal is to the heart and will. The book is committed to the press with the prayer that the reality of the Kingdom of God may bring blessing to many readers, as it has to the author.

GEORGE ELDON LADD.

Pasadena, California.

CONTENTS

INTRODUCTION

ESCHATOLOGY has always been a fascinating subject. It appeals to both Christian and non-Christian alike. Everyone is curious about the future. That is why we have always had so many magicians and fortune-tellers. Especially today do men long to know what lies ahead. However, apart from the Word of God we can only speculate. It alone discloses God's purpose both for the present and the future.

I have read many books on prophecy. I am familiar with the various schools of thought and interpretation. Much has been written about the Kingdom of God. But of all the books I have read, I have never come across one that so clearly and so Scripturally deals with the Kingdom as does Dr. Ladd's new volume, *The Gospel of the Kingdom*.

Dr. Ladd shows that the Kingdom of God belongs to the present as well as the future. He conceives of the Kingdom as the rule, the reign, the government of God in this age in the hearts and lives of those who yield themselves to Him, and in the next age over all the world. He sums it up in the second chapter in this way:

"The Kingdom of God is basically the rule of God. It is God's reign, the divine sovereignty in action. God's reign, however, is manifested in several realms, and the Gospels speak of entering into the Kingdom of God both today and tomorrow. God's reign manifests itself both in the future and in the present and thereby creates both a future realm and a present realm in which man may experience the blessings of His reign."

His interpretation of the parables is most illuminating. He does not believe that an interpretation has to be found for every detail. His understanding is that the Kingdom, though insignificant in appearance at present, is a reality and that it is destined to dominate the whole world. God will some day rule over all. This is a conception quite different from the usual interpretations given by the various schools of prophetic study. It should encourage the discouraged and give hope to the hopeless. God's government regardless of appearances is bound to triumph at last. Nothing can withstand it.

Dr. Ladd's interpretation of the Sermon on the Mount is the clearest I have ever read. No one can study it without being deeply convicted. It cuts squarely across the practices and teachings of our day. Divorce, lust, anger, oaths, etc., are dealt with in no uncertain way. The interpretation is evangelistic and Scriptural in every sense of the word. It will make the Bible a new book.

It seems to me that the author's emphasis on the absolute necessity of a decision with all that it involves is of the utmost importance. Dr. Ladd does not minimize the cost. Discipleship always costs. There is a price to pay. The rich young ruler had to give up all. God's government demands complete submission. His subjects must put Him first. The Kingdom is entered only when a decision has been made and the price paid.

Then too, he makes it clear that the Church is to preach the Gospel of the Kingdom right up to the end of the age, and that only when the task has been completed will the King return.

It is my hope that this book will be studied by ministers, students, and Christian workers everywhere. I congratulate Dr. Ladd upon having written it. He has made a real contribution to the Church in our day.

OSWALD J. SMITH

Los Angeles
February, 1959

_65_

CHAPTER I

WHAT IS THE KINGDOM OF GOD?

WE live in a wonderful and yet a fearful day. It is a wonderful day because of the amazing accomplishments of our modern scientific skills which have provided us with a measure of comfort and prosperity undreamed of a century ago. Great metal birds soar through the air, swallowing up thousands of miles in a few hours. Floating palaces bring to the ocean voyager all the luxuries of the most elegant hotel. The automobile has freed man to explore for himself scenes and sights which to his grandparents were contained only in story-books. Electrical power has brought a score of slaves to serve the humblest housewife. Medical science has conquered the plague, smallpox, and other scourges of physical well-being and is on the threshold of other amazing conquests.

A marvellous age, indeed! Yet happiness and security seem further removed than ever, for we face dangers and hazards of unparalleled dimensions. We have come victoriously through a war in which the foundations of human liberty were threatened; yet the columns of our newspapers are stained with unbelievable stories of the suppression of human freedom, and the fight for freedom goes on. New discoveries in the structure of matter have opened unimaginable vistas of blessing for man's physical well-being; yet these very discoveries hold the potential, in the hands of evil men, of blasting society from the face of the earth.

In a day like this, wonderful yet fearful, men are asking questions. What does it all mean? Where are we going? What is the meaning and the goal of human history? Men are concerned today not only about the individual and the destiny of his soul but also about the meaning of history itself. Does mankind have a destiny? Or do we jerk across the stage of time like wooden puppets, only to have the stage, the actors, and the theatre itself

13

destroyed by fire, leaving only a pile of ashes and the smell of smoke?

In ancient times, poets and seers longed for an ideal society. Hesiod dreamed of a lost Golden Age in the distant past but saw no brightness in the present, constant care for the morrow, and no hope for the future. Plato pictured an ideal state organized on philosophical principles; but he himself realized that his plan was too idealistic to be realized. Virgil sang of one who would deliver the world from its sufferings and by whom "the great line of the ages begins anew."

The Hebrew-Christian faith expresses its hope in terms of the Kingdom of God. This Biblical hope is not in the same category as the dreams of the Greek poets but is at the very heart of revealed religion. The Biblical idea of the Kingdom of God is deeply rooted in the Old Testament and is grounded in the confidence that there is one eternal, living God who has revealed Himself to men and who has a purpose for the human race which He has chosen to accomplish through Israel. The Biblical hope is therefore a religious hope; it is an essential element in the revealed will and the redemptive work of the living God.

Thus the prophets announced a day when men will live together in peace. God shall then "judge between the nations, and shall decide for many peoples; and they shall beat their swords into plowshares, and their spears into pruning hooks; nation shall not lift up sword against nation, neither shall they learn war any more" (Isa. 2: 4). Not only shall the problems of human society be solved, but the evils of man's physical environment shall be no more. "The wolf shall dwell with the lamb, and the leopard shall lie down with the kid, and the calf and the young lion and the fatling together, and a little child shall lead them" (Isa. 11: 6). Peace, safety, security—all this was promised for the happy future.

Then came Jesus of Nazareth with the announcement, "Repent, for the kingdom of heaven is at hand" (Matt. 4: 17). This theme of the coming of the Kingdom of God was central in His mission. His teaching was designed to show men how they might enter the Kingdom of God (Matt. 5: 20; 7: 21). His mighty works were intended to prove that the Kingdom of God had come upon them (Matt. 12: 28). His parables illustrated to His disciples the truth about the Kingdom of God (Matt. 13: 11). And when He taught His followers to pray, at the heart of their petition were the words, "Thy kingdom come, thy will be done on earth as it is in heaven" (Matt. 6: 10). On the eve of His death, He assured His disciples that He would yet share with them the happiness and the fellowship of the Kingdom (Luke 22: 22-30). And He promised that He would appear again on the earth in glory to bring the blessedness of the Kingdom to those for whom it was prepared (Matt. 25: 31, 34).

When we ask the Christian Church, "What is the Kingdom of God? When and how will it come?" we receive a bewildering diversity of explanations. There are few themes so prominent in the Bible which have received such radically divergent interpretations as that of the Kingdom of God.

Some, like Adolf von Harnack, reduced the Kingdom of God to the subjective realm and understood it in terms of the human spirit and its relationship to God. The Kingdom of God is an inward power which enters into the human soul and lays hold of it. It consists of a few basic religious truths of universal application. The more recent interpretation of C. H. Dodd, conceives of the Kingdom as the absolute, the "wholly other" which has entered into time and space in the person of Jesus of Nazareth.

At the other extreme are those who, like Albert Schweitzer, define Jesus' message of the Kingdom as an apocalyptic realm to be inaugurated by a supernatural act of God when history will be broken off and a new heavenly order of existence begun. The Kingdom of God in no sense of the word is a present or a spiritual reality; it is altogether future and supernatural.

Another type of interpretation relates the Kingdom of God in one way or another to the Church. Since the days of Augustine, the Kingdom has been identified with the Church. As the Church grows, the Kingdom grows and is extended in the world. Many Protestant theologians have taught a modified form of this interpretation, holding that the Kingdom of God may be identified with the true Church which is embodied in the visible professing Church. As the Church takes the Gospel into all the world, it extends the Kingdom of God. An optimistic version holds that it is the mission of the Church to win the entire world to Christ and thus transform the world into the Kingdom of God. The Gospel is the supernatural redeeming Gospel of Jesus Christ, and the Kingdom is to be established by the Church's proclamation of the Gospel. The Gospel must not only offer a personal salvation in the future life to those who believe; it must also transform all of the relationships of life here and now and thus cause the Kingdom of God to prevail in all the world. The Gospel of redeeming grace has the power to save the social, economic and political orders as well as the souls of individual believers. The Kingdom of God is like a bit of leaven placed in a bowl of dough which slowly but steadily permeates the dough until the entire lump is leavened. So is the Kingdom of God to transform the world by slow and gradual permeation.

Still others have understood the Kingdom of God to be essentially an ideal pattern for human society. The Kingdom is not primarily concerned with individual salvation or with the future but with the social problems of the present. Men build the Kingdom of God as they work for the ideal social order and endeavour to solve the problems of poverty, sickness, labour relations, social inequalities and race relationships. The primary task of the Church is to build the Kingdom of God. Those who are interested in the history of interpretation will find a brief but comprehensive survey with documentation in the author's book, *Crucial Questions About the Kingdom of God* (Grand Rapids: Eerdmans, 1952).

In the face of such diversity of interpretation in the history of Christian theology, many readers will react by saying, "Let us be done with all human interpretations. Let us go directly to the Word of God and find what it has to say about the Kingdom of God." The perplexing fact is that when we turn to the Scriptures, we find an almost equally bewildering diversity of statements about the Kingdom of God. If you will take a concordance of the Bible, look up every reference in the New Testament alone where the word "kingdom" occurs, write down a brief summary of each verse on a piece of paper, you will probably find yourself at a loss to know what to do with the complexity of teaching.

The Word of God *does* say that the Kingdom of God is a present spiritual reality. "For the kingdom of God is not eating and drinking but righteousness and peace and joy in the Holy Spirit" (Rom. 14: 17). Righteousness and peace and joy are fruits of the Spirit which God bestows now upon those who yield their

lives to the rule of the Spirit. They have to do with the deepest
springs of the spiritual life, and this, says the inspired apostle, is the
Kingdom of God.

At the same time, the Kingdom is an inheritance which God
will bestow upon His people when Christ comes in glory. "Then
the King will say to those on his right hand, 'Come, O blessed of
my Father, inherit the kingdom prepared for you from the
foundation of the world'" (Matt. 25: 34). How can the Kingdom
of God be a present spiritual reality and yet be an inheritance
bestowed upon God's people at the Second Coming of Christ?

Another facet of Kingdom truth reflects the fact that the Kingdom is a realm into which the followers of Jesus Christ have
entered. Paul writes that God has "delivered us from the dominion of darkness and transferred us to the kingdom of his beloved
Son" (Col. 1: 13). This verse makes it very clear that the redeemed
are already in the Kingdom of Christ. It may of course be objected
that we must distinguish between the Kingdom of God and the
Kingdom of Christ; but this seems impossible, for the Kingdom
of God is also the Kingdom of Christ (Eph. 5: 5; Rev. 11: 15).
Furthermore, our Lord describes those who received His message
and mission as those who *now* enter into the Kingdom of God
(Luke 16: 16).

At the same time, the Kingdom of God is a future realm which
we must enter when Christ returns. Peter looks to a future day
when there "will be richly provided for you an entrance into the
eternal kingdom of our Lord and Saviour Jesus Christ" (II Pet.
1: 11). Our Lord Himself frequently referred to this future event.
"Many will come from the east and west and sit at table with
Abraham, Isaac, and Jacob in the kingdom of heaven" (Matt.
8: 11).

This future coming of the Kingdom will be attended with
great glory. Jesus told of the day when the angels "will gather
out of his kingdom all causes of sin and all evildoers. . . . Then the
righteous will shine like the sun in the kingdom of their Father"
(Matt. 13: 41, 43). On the other hand, when asked by the
Pharisees when the Kingdom of God was coming, he answered,
"The kingdom of God is not coming with signs to be observed;
nor will they say, 'Lo, here it is!' or, 'There!' for behold, the
kingdom of God is in the midst of you' (Luke 17: 20–21). The

B

Kingdom is already present in the midst of men; and Jesus flatly discouraged the Pharisees from looking for a future Kingdom which would come with an outward display of glory.

The parables of the Kingdom make it clear that in some sense, the Kingdom is present and at work in the world. The Kingdom of God *is* like a tiny seed which becomes a great tree; it *is* like leaven which will one day have permeated the entire bowl of dough (Luke 13: 18-21). Yet on the other hand, when Pilate examined Jesus about His teaching, Jesus replied, "My kingdom is not of this world" (John 18: 36).

The very complexity of the Biblical teaching about the Kingdom of God is one of the reasons why such diverse interpretations have arisen in the history of theology. Isolated verses can be quoted for most of the interpretations which can be found in our theological literature. The Kingdom is a present reality (Matt. 12: 28), and yet it is a future blessing (I Cor. 15: 50). It is an inner spiritual redemptive blessing (Rom. 14: 17) which can be experienced only by way of the new birth (John 3: 3), and yet it will have to do with the government of the nations of the world (Rev. 11: 15). The Kingdom is a realm into which men enter now (Matt. 21: 31), and yet it is a realm into which they will enter tomorrow (Matt. 8: 11). It is at the same time a gift of God which will be bestowed by God in the future (Luke 12: 32) and yet which must be received in the present (Mark 10: 15). Obviously no simple explanation can do justice to such a rich but diverse variety of teaching.

There is, however, a basic solution to this complex problem which will provide a key of meaning to open the door into treasures of understanding and blessing. This key provides the simplest approach to this involved and diverse body of Scriptural truth. It is a key which is often overlooked because of the difference between modern and ancient idiom.

We must ask the most fundamental question: What is the meaning of "kingdom"? The modern answer to this question loses the key of meaning to this ancient Biblical truth. In our western idiom, a kingdom is primarily a realm over which a king exercises his authority. Not many kingdoms remain in our modern world with its democratic interests; but we think of the United Kingdom of Great Britain and Northern Ireland as the original group of countries which recognize the Queen as their sovereign. The dictionary follows this line of thought by giving as its first modern definition, "A state or monarchy the head of which is a king; dominion; realm."

The second meaning of a kingdom is the people belonging to a given realm. The Kingdom of Great Britain may be thought of as the citizens over whom the Queen exercises her rule, the subjects of her kingdom.

The exclusive application of either of these two ideas to the Biblical teaching of the Kingdom leads us astray from a correct understanding of the Biblical truth. The English dictionary itself makes this mistake when it gives as the theological definition of the kingdom, "The spiritual realm having God as its head." This definition cannot do justice to the verses which speak of the coming of the Kingdom in outward glory and power when Christ returns. On the other hand, those who begin with the idea of a future realm inaugurated by the return of Christ cannot do justice to the sayings about the Kingdom as a present spiritual reality.

Furthermore, those who begin with the idea of the Kingdom as a people base their definition upon the identity of the Kingdom with the Church, and for this there is very little scriptural warrant.

We must set aside our modern idiom if we are to understand Biblical terminology. At this point Webster's dictionary provides us with a clue when it gives as its first definition: "The rank, quality, state, or attributes of a king; royal authority; dominion; monarchy; kingship. *Archaic*." From the viewpoint of modern linguistic usage, this definition may be archaic; but it is precisely this archaism which is necessary to understand the ancient Biblical teaching. The *primary* meaning of both the Hebrew word *malkuth* in the Old Testament and of the Greek word *basileia* in the New Testament is the rank, authority and sovereignty exercised by a king. A *basileia* may indeed be a realm over which a sovereign exercises his authority; and it may be the people who belong to that realm and over whom authority is exercised; but these are secondary and derived meanings. First of all, a kingdom is the authority to rule, the sovereignty of the king.

This primary meaning of the word "kingdom" may be seen in its Old Testament use to describe a king's rule. Ezra 8: 1 speaks of the return from Babylon "in the kingdom" of Artaxerxes, *i.e.,* his reign. II Chronicles 12: 1 speaks of the establishment of Rehoboam's kingdom or rule. Daniel 8: 23 refers to the latter end of their kingdom or rule. This usage of "kingdom" as a human reign may also be found in such passages as Jeremiah 49: 34; II Chronicles 11: 17, 12: 1, 26: 30; Ezra 4: 5; Nehemiah 12: 22, etc.

When the word refers to God's Kingdom, it always refers to His reign, His rule, His sovereignty, and not to the realm in which it is exercised. Psalm 103: 19, "The Lord has established his throne in the heavens, and his kingdom rules over all." God's kingdom, His *malkuth*, is His universal rule, His sovereignty over all the earth. Psalm 145: 11, "They shall speak of the glory of thy kingdom, and tell of thy power." In the parallelism of Hebrew poetry, the two lines express the same truth. God's Kingdom is His power. Psalm 145: 13, "Thy kingdom is an everlasting kingdom, and thy dominion endures throughout all generations." The *realm* of God's rule is the heaven and earth, but this verse has no reference to the permanence of this realm. It is God's rule which is everlasting. Daniel 2: 37, "You, O king, the king of kings, to whom the God of heaven has given the kingdom, the power, and the might, and the glory." Notice the synonyms for kingdom: power, might, glory—all expressions of authority. These terms identify the Kingdom as the "rule" which God has given to the king. Of Belshazzar, it was written, "God has numbered the days of your kingdom and brought it to an end" (Dan. 5: 26). It is clear that the realm over which Belshazzar ruled was not destroyed. The Babylonian *realm* and *people* were not brought to an end; they were transferred to another ruler. It was the rule of the king which was terminated, and it was the rule which was given to Darius the Mede (Dan. 5: 31).

One reference in our Gospels makes this meaning very clear. We read in Luke 19: 11-12, "As they heard these things, he proceeded to tell a parable, because he was near to Jerusalem, and because they supposed that the kingdom of God was to appear immediately. He said therefore, 'A nobleman went into a far country to receive a *basileia* and then return.'" The nobleman did not go away to get a realm, an area over which to rule. The realm over which he wanted to reign was at hand. The territory over which he was to rule was this place he left. The problem was that he was no king. He needed authority, the right to rule. He went off to get a "kingdom," *i.e., kingship,* authority. The Revised Standard Version has therefore translated the word "kingly power."

This very thing had happened some years before the days of our Lord. In the year 40 B.C. political conditions in Palestine had become chaotic. The Romans had subdued the country in 63 B.C., but stability had been slow in coming. Herod the Great finally went to Rome, obtained from the Roman Senate the kingdom, and was declared to be king. He literally went into a far country to receive a kingship, the authority to be king in Judaea over the Jews. It may well be that our Lord had this incident in mind in this parable. In any case, it illustrates the fundamental meaning of kingdom.

The Kingdom of God is His kingship, His rule, His authority. When this is once realized, we can go through the New Testament and find passage after passage where this meaning is evident, where the Kingdom is not a realm or a people but God's reign. Jesus said that we must "receive the kingdom of God" as little children (Mark 10: 15). What is received? The Church? Heaven? What is received is God's rule. In order to enter the future realm of the Kingdom, one must submit himself in perfect trust to God's rule here and now.

We must also "seek first his kingdom and his righteousness" (Matt. 6: 33). What is the object of our quest? The Church? Heaven? No; we are to seek God's righteousness—His sway, His rule, His reign in our lives.

When we pray, "Thy kingdom come,' are we praying for heaven to come to earth? In a sense we are praying for this; but heaven is an object of desire only because the reign of God is to be more perfectly realized then it is now. Apart from the reign of God, heaven is meaningless. Therefore, what we pray for is, "Thy kingdom come; *thy will be done* on earth as it is in heaven." This prayer is a petition for God to reign, to manifest His kingly sovereignty and power, to put to flight every enemy of righteousness and of His divine rule, that God alone may be King over all the world.

However, a reign without a realm in which it is exercised is meaningless. Thus we find that the Kingdom of God is also the realm in which God's reign may be experienced. But again, the Biblical facts are not simple. Sometimes the Bible speaks of the Kingdom as the realm into which we enter as present, sometimes as though it were future.

It is future in such verses as Mark 9: 47, "It is better for you to enter the kingdom of God with one eye than with two eyes to be thrown into hell." (See also Mark 10: 23, 14: 25, Matt. 7: 21.) In such passages the Kingdom of God is equivalent to that aspect of eternal life which will be experienced only after the Second Coming of Christ.

In other passages, the Kingdom is present and may be entered here and now. Luke 16: 16, "The law and the prophets were until John; since then the good news of the kingdom of God is preached, and every one enters it violently." Matt. 21: 31, "The tax collectors and the harlots go into the kingdom of God before you." Luke 11: 52, "Woe to you lawyers! for you have taken away the key of knowledge: you did not enter yourselves, and you hindered those who were entering."

Our problem, then, is found in this threefold fact: (1) Some passages of Scripture refer to the Kingdom of God as God's reign. (2) Some passages refer to God's Kingdom as the realm into which we may now enter to experience the blessings of His reign. (3) Still other passages refer to a future realm which will come only with the return of our Lord Jesus Christ into which we shall then enter and experience the fulness of His reign. Thus the Kingdom of God means three different things in different verses. One has to study all the references in the light of their context and then try to fit them together in an overall interpretation.

Fundamentally, as we have seen, the Kingdom of God is God's sovereign reign; but God's reign expresses itself in different stages through redemptive history. Therefore, men may enter into the realm of God's reign in its several stages of manifestation and experience the blessings of His reign in differing degrees. God's Kingdom is the realm of the Age to Come, popularly called heaven; then we shall realize the blessings of His Kingdom (reign) in the perfection of their fulness. But the Kingdom is here now. There is a realm of spiritual blessing into which we may enter today and enjoy in part but in reality the blessings of God's Kingdom (reign).

We pray, "Thy Kingdom come, Thy will be done on earth as it is in heaven." The confidence that this prayer is to be answered when God brings human history to the divinely ordained consummation enables the Christian to retain his balance and sanity of mind in this mad world in which we live. Our hearts go out to those who have no such hope. Thank God, His Kingdom is coming, and it will fill all the earth.

But when we pray, "Thy Kingdom come," we also ask that God's will be done here and now, today. This is the primary concern of these expositions, that the reader might meet the Kingdom of God, or rather, that the Kingdom of God might meet him. We should also pray, "Thy kingdom come, Thy will be done" in my church as it is in heaven. The life and fellowship of a Christian church ought to be a fellowship of people among whom God's will is done—a bit of heaven on earth. "Thy kingdom come, Thy will be done" in my life, as it is in heaven. This is included in our prayer for the coming of the Kingdom. This is part of the Gospel of the Kingdom of God.

CHAPTER II

THE KINGDOM IS TOMORROW

IN our introductory chapter, we sketched several prevailing interpretations of the Kingdom of God and then attempted a basic description. The Kingdom of God is basically the rule of God. It is God's reign, the divine sovereignty in action. God's reign, however, is manifested in several realms, and the Gospels speak of entering into the Kingdom of God both today and tomorrow. God's reign manifests itself both in the future and in the present and thereby creates both a future realm and a present realm in which men may experience the blessings of His reign.

The Kingdom of God is, then, the realization of God's will and the enjoyment of the accompanying blessings. However, it is a clear teaching of the New Testament that God's will is not to be *perfectly* realized in this age. Central in Biblical Theology is the doctrine of the Second Coming of Jesus Christ. Schweitzer was to this extent right, that the so-called apocalyptic or "other-worldly" aspect of the Kingdom of God is not an extraneous appendage which can be sloughed off without impairing the Biblical teaching. The Bible conceives of the entire sweep of human history as resting in the hand of God, but it looks for the final realization of God's Kingdom in a realm "beyond history," *i.e.,* in a new and different order of existence.

Yet while this is true, there is a very real and a very vital sense in which God has already manifested His reign, His will, His Kingdom, in the coming of Christ in the flesh, by virtue of which we may experience the life of the Kingdom here and now. As there are two advents of Christ, one in the flesh which we call the Incarnation, the other in glory which we call the *Parousia* or Second Advent, so there are two manifestations of God's Kingdom: one in power and glory when Christ returns, but one which is present now because God's Son has already appeared among men. In this chapter, we are concerned to ascertain what the New Testament tells us about the future aspect of His reign; but throughout the rest of the book we shall devote ourselves to the present aspect of God's Kingdom as it has to do with present experience.

In order to understand this theme and to appreciate how the Kingdom of God can both be future and present, we need to sketch this truth against the background of another Biblical teaching which has been infrequently emphasized and may seem to some quite novel. In popular Christian idiom, we often contrast the life of the present with that of the future by use of the words earth and heaven. We live our bodily life here on earth, but the future salvation will be consummated in heaven. A more philosophical approach contrasts time and eternity as though they represented two different modes of existence. Our present life is lived "in time" while the future order will be "beyond time" in eternity. This concept is reflected in our popular religious idiom in the song:

> *When the trumpet of the Lord shall sound* and time shall be no more,
> *When the morning breaks eternal,* bright and fair . . .

One of the most brilliant recent discussions in Biblical Theology is that of Oscar Cullmann in which he successfully demonstrated that such concepts are foreign to the Biblical view. His book, *Christ and Time*,[1] has shown that the Biblical world-view involves a linear concept, and that "eternity" as it belongs to redemptive history is simply unending time. This fact is obscured in both the Authorized or King James Version and in the Revised Version, which mistranslate the word underlying this Biblical world-view. There are two words in the Greek New Testament which are translated by the single English word "world"—a fact which is obscured in our older English versions. First, there is the Greek word *kosmos*. A *kosmos* is something which is in proper order or harmony, something which enjoys proper arrangement. Our word "cosmetics" is derived from this Greek word. Cosmetics are aids for the ladies in arranging their faces, to put them in proper order, to adorn them. *Kosmos* in its most common Greek usage is the world as the sum and total of everything constituting an orderly universe.

[1] Philadelphia: Westminster, 1950, London: S.C.M. Press, 1951.

However, there is another word which is often grievously mistranslated in our Authorized Version. This word is *aion*, from which the English word æon is derived. Primarily, *aion* has no connotation of an order or a structure but designates a period of time and ought to be translated by the English word "age."

When we trace this word in the New Testament, we discover that in the course of God's redemptive purpose, there are two ages which are frequently called "This Age" and "The Age to Come." In Matthew 12: 32 the A.V. reads, "Whosoever speaketh a word against the Son of man, it shall be forgiven him: but whosoever speaketh against the Holy Ghost, it shall not be forgiven him, neither in this world, neither in the world to come." However, our Lord is not speaking of two worlds but of two ages. The entire sweep of man's existence is set forth in terms of this age and the age which is to come. The Greek word used is not *kosmos* but *aion*, age. It is unfortunate that our older English Bibles obscure this important fact; but it is correctly rendered in the R.S.V.[1] Blasphemy against the Son of Man will be forgiven, but blasphemy against the Holy Spirit will *never* be forgiven; and the sweep of "never" is two periods of time: This Age, and that which is to come.

In Ephesians 1: 21, Paul describes the exaltation of Christ "far above all rule and authority and power and dominion, and above every name that is named, not only in this age but also in that which is to come." Here again the A.V.'s translation "world" is inaccurate. Paul does not have in mind two worlds but two ages. His word is not *kosmos* but *aion*. There is no thought of two orders of society but of two periods of time.

A slight variant of this expression is found in Mark 10: 29, 30, "Jesus said, 'Truly, I say to you, there is no one who has left house or brethren or sisters or mother or father or children or lands, for my sake and for the gospel, who will not receive a hundredfold now in this time, houses and brothers and sisters and mothers and children and lands, with persecution, and in the age to come eternal life.'" In the second half of the verse, we

---

[1] We recognize that there is at times an overlapping of meaning between the two words, due in part to the fact that both are used to render the one Hebrew word *olam*. In Heb. 1: 2; 11: 3, *aion* is nearly synonymous with *kosmos*. However, in most instances *aion* retains the temporal idea.

find again the word *aion*; and the translation "in the world to come" does not accurately represent the idea. In the first half of the verse, the word "time" (*kairos*) appears instead of *aion* or age. This makes it doubly clear that the reference of the verse is to two periods of time, not to two worlds. In this time, in This Age, we are to expect hostility to the Gospel. In The Age to Come, those who have followed Christ will be freed from all opposition and sufferings and will enjoy eternal life.

When we trace this concept further, we discover that these two ages are separated by the Second Coming of Christ and the resurrection from the dead. In Matthew 24: 3, the disciples came to Jesus with the question, "Tell us, when will this be, and what shall be the sign of your coming and of the close of the age?" The rendering of both the A.V. and the R.V. suggests that the disciples were asking about the time of the destruction of this world—its end. On the contrary, their question had to do with the consummation of This Age which will be followed by another age. According to this verse, This Age is expected to come to its close with the *Parousia* or Second Coming of Christ, and it will be followed by The Age to Come.[1]

Another event dividing This Age from The Age to Come is the resurrection from the dead. In Luke 20: 34–36 we read, "Jesus said to them, 'The sons of this age marry and are given in marriage; but those who are accounted worthy to attain to that age and to the resurrection from the dead neither marry nor are given in marriage.'" Here again, our Lord refers to the two ages, not two worlds. In This Age, marriage is a necessary institution. "The sons of This Age"—all who live in this time—must marry and raise children to propagate the race. But a different state of affairs will prevail in The Age to Come, for those who enter that Age will do so by way of resurrection. Therefore, they will be like the angels in this one respect: they no longer will be subject to death but will, like the angels, be immortal, for they have become "sons of the resurrection." Therefore, not only the Second Coming of Christ but also the resurrection from the dead will terminate This Age and inaugurate The Age to Come.

[1] The disciples' question was concerned both with the fall of Jerusalem and the eschatological consummation of the age, but this involves a difficult problem which cannot here be discussed.

We may illustrate this basic structure by a simple diagram which we shall designate "The Conflict of the Ages."

C stands for creation, P for the *Parousia* of Christ, and R for the resurrection of the dead.[1] This Age had its beginning with creation, but The Age to Come will go on endlessly, for ever. We may therefore speak of The Age to Come as Eternity, by which we mean unending time. This simple time line is shared by the writers of the New Testament with contemporary Judaism, for both are rooted in the Old Testament world-view.

When we ask what Scripture teaches about the character of these two ages, we find a sharp contrast. This Age is dominated by evil, wickedness, and rebellion against the will of God, while The Age to Come is the age of the Kingdom of God.

In Galatians 1: 4 we read that Christ "gave himself for our sins that he might deliver us from the present evil age." This Age is an evil age; it is characterized by sin and unrighteousness. It is an age from which men need deliverance, a deliverance which can be accomplished only by the death of Christ.

The second chapter of Ephesians gives us an extended discussion of the character of This Age. Paul says, "And you he made alive, when you were dead through the trespasses and sins in which you once walked, following the age of this world" (Eph. 2: 1–2).[2] In this verse, both words "age" and "world" are employed, indicating that while This Age and the world are not synonymous, they are closely related. There is a certain order of human society which characterizes This Age. Paul describes it with the words, "In which you once walked . . . following the prince of the power of the air, the spirit that is now at work in the sons of disobedience." The character of the age of this world bears the stamp of the Prince of the power of the air, that is, Satan. He is permitted to exercise a terrible influence throughout This

---

[1] Cullmann conceives of time as extending backwards before creation (*Christ and Time*, p. 82), but this raises a philosophical question about which the Scriptures are silent.

[2] We have here given a literal rendition of the Greek.

Age inducing men and women to walk in a way displeasing to God.

"Among these we all once lived in the passions of our flesh, following the desires of the body and mind, and so we were by nature children of wrath, like the rest of mankind." These passions of the flesh are not alone bodily, "fleshy" sins; they are not only sins of gluttony and of drunkenness and of immorality. Pride is a sin of the flesh. So are egotism, selfishness, stubbornness, determination to have one's own way (Gal. 5: 19-21). All of these belong to "the flesh." When we were walking according to This Age, we lived according to the lusts of our flesh and were by nature children of wrath. This is a terrible verse. "Children of wrath . . ." God's wrath, the holy judgment of a righteous God rests upon This Age, upon its sinfulness and its rebellion. God's wrath must also fall inescapably upon those who are conformed to its evil, rebellious character.

In the parable of the soils, we read of seed which falls upon thorny ground. The seed sprouts but the thorns grow up and choke the growth (Matt. 13: 7). Our Lord interprets this with the words, "As for what was sown among thorns, this is he who hears the word, but the care of the age and the delight in riches choke the word, and it proves unfruitful" (Matt. 13: 22). The care of the age is not alone worry and the trouble and anxiety of making a living. It is the entire spirit which characterizes This Age: worry and anxiety about one's physical life to be sure, but also the pressure, the drive of ambition for wealth, success, prosperity, and power. All of this is involved in the care, the burden, of This Age.

The point is this: it is the character of This Age to choke the working of the Word of God. The spirit of the Age is hostile to the Gospel. When the Gospel is preached, it often seems to lodge in the hearts of men and women. They hear it, they seem to receive it, they make a response to it. And yet it is often only a superficial response. There is no fruit. As the care, the concern of the Age presses in upon them, they are not willing to pay the price of following Christ. The Word of God is choked and is unfruitful. This Age is hostile to the Gospel, and men often yield in conformity to This Age rather than surrender to the claims of the Gospel. There is a conflict between the Age and the Gospel of the Kingdom.

One of the most important verses describing This Age is II Cor. 4: 3–4 because it explains what lies behind these other sayings. "And even if our gospel is veiled, it is veiled only to those who are perishing. In their case the god of this age has blinded the minds of the unbelievers, to keep them from seeing the light of the gospel of the glory of Christ."

Two things stand out in this verse. Satan is the "god of this age." In God's sovereign purpose, Satan has been permitted to exercise a great measure of authority and power throughout the duration of This Age. We have already read in Ephesians that in the age of this world, we once lived according to the prince of the power of the air. As an instrument of His judicial righteousness, God has permitted Satan to exercise such influence in This Age that Paul can speak of him as though he were the god of This Age. Whence comes the evil, the hatred, the deception, the strife, the conflict, the sin, the misery, and the pain, suffering and dying which characterize This Age? It comes from Satan. This does not mean that man can throw off responsibility for his own evil conduct. Man remains a free moral agent and is answerable both before the judgment of God and his fellow men. It does mean that evil is more than human. It has its source in an evil, superhuman personality. This fact is not to be interpreted as a fundamental dualism as though God and Satan, good and evil, were two eternal principles. Back of all things, including Satan and evil, stands the eternal God. But God has permitted Satan to wield such power that the result is a limited ethical dualism.

We can discover in II Cor. 4: 4 the manifestation of satanic influence. It is not found in the fact that the "god of this age" has dragged good men down into the gutter of sin, or that strong young men and beautiful young women have been thrown down into a sink of immorality and corruption. "In their case the god of this age hath *blinded* the minds of the unbelievers, to keep them from seeing the light of the gospel of the glory of Christ."

Here is the root of evil: blindness, darkness, unbelief. The Biblical philosophy of sin makes ethical and moral evil secondary to religious evil. Paul elsewhere refers to the "ungodliness and wickedness of men" (Rom. 1: 18). All forms of wickedness ultimately grow out of the root of ungodliness. Sin is primarily religious and secondarily ethical. Man is God's creature and his primary responsibility is towards God. The root of sin is found in his refusal to acknowledge in grateful dependence the gifts and the goodness of God (Rom. 1: 21), which are now imparted in Christ. Darkness is the assertion of independence rather than God-dependence.

The primary manifestation of satanic influence and of the evil of This Age is religious; it is blindness with reference to the Gospel of Jesus Christ. How often we fail to understand satanic devices! A man may be a cultured, ethical and even religious person and yet be in demonic darkness. Satan's basic desire is to keep men from Christ. His primary concern is not to corrupt morals nor to make atheists nor to produce enemies of religion. Indeed religion which rests upon the assumption of human adequacy and sufficiency is an enemy of the light. This is the character of the Age of this world: darkness.

It is obvious from these verses that the Kingdom of God does not belong to This Age, for Satan is called the god of This Age. This is not to suggest that God has been dethroned or His hand removed from the control of the universe. It remains eternally true that "The Lord has established his throne in the heavens, and his kingdom rules over all" (Ps. 103: 19). Even when evil is strongest on the earth, when God's people are most violently attacked by Satan, God is still the "King of the ages" (Rev. 15: 3).[1] It is in the providence of God's sovereign rule that this state of affairs has come to pass. It is, however, basic to our understanding of the Kingdom of God to recognize the Biblical teaching that This Age is in rebellion against God's rule.

The New Testament sets The Age to Come in direct opposition to This Age. The present age is evil, but the Kingdom of God belongs to The Age to Come. The Kingdom of God, both as the perfect manifestation of God's reign and the realm of completed redemptive blessing, belongs to The Age to Come.

This is clearly illustrated in our Lord's conversation with the rich young ruler who came with the request, "Teacher, what good deed must I do to have eternal life?" (Matt. 19: 16). This young

---

[1] This is the best rendering, although variant texts read "saints" or "nations."

man was not acquainted with the teaching that a man can have eternal life here and now. He was interested in life in The Age to Come. Our Lord told him he should free himself of every restraint that hindered him from becoming a disciple. "When the young man heard this, he went away sorrowful; for he had great possessions" (v. 22).

Then "Jesus said unto his disciples, 'Truly, I say to you, it will be hard for a rich man to enter the kingdom of heaven.'" The young man's question was, "How may I have eternal life?" Our Lord's answer was, "It will be hard for a rich man to enter the kingdom of heaven" (v. 23). "And again I tell you, it is easier for a camel to go through the eye of a needle than for a rich man to enter the kingdom of God" (v. 24).

In passing, let us notice that these two phrases, "the Kingdom of God" and "the Kingdom of Heaven" are obviously interchangeable. Furthermore, "the Kingdom of God" and "the Kingdom of Heaven" are both interchangeable with eternal life. Mark, Luke, and John always speak of the Kingdom of God, Matthew alone has the Kingdom of Heaven; and in 12: 28; 19: 24; 21: 31, 43, Matthew has the Kingdom of God. The difference between the two phrases is to be explained on linguistic grounds. The Kingdom of Heaven is the Semitic form and the Kingdom of God is the Greek form of the same phrase. Our Lord taught in Aramaic, a language very similar to Hebrew, whereas our New Testament is written in Greek. Jesus, teaching Jews, probably spoke of "the Kingdom of the Heavens" which would be the natural Jewish form of expression. We have extensive evidence from Jewish rabbinic literature that this phrase was in common usage. To the Greek ear, these words would be meaningless; and when the phrase was translated in our Greek Gospels for Greek readers, it was uniformly rendered "the Kingdom of God." In the Gospel of Matthew, which was probably written to Jewish believers, the original phrase "the Kingdom of the Heavens" was usually retained. The terminology in Matthew 19: 23-24 makes it quite clear that the two phrases are interchangeable and that no difference of meaning is to be sought between them.

What did the Lord mean in saying that it is easier for a camel to go through a needle's eye than for a rich man to enter into the

Kingdom of God? What is the Kingdom of God? In verse 23, it is the Kingdom of Heaven. In verse 16, it is eternal life. Then the disciples asked, "Who then can be saved?" (v. 25). Clearly, all of these expressions refer to the same blessing to be obtained in the future when Christ comes again. The Kingdom of God, the Kingdom of Heaven, eternal life, salvation: they are interchangeable terms. Jesus says that with men, it is *impossible* to be saved. Entrance into eternal life in the Kingdom of God is no more possible for men to attain by all human resources than it is possible for a camel to go through a needle's eye. This would be a miracle indeed. And so is it a miracle for a rich man—or a poor man either for that matter—to have his affections turned from his possessions that he may become a disciple of Jesus and thus be prepared to enter the future Kingdom of Heaven.

But for those who have experienced this miracle in their lives, Jesus gave the promise, "Truly, I say to you, in the new world when the Son of man shall sit on his glorious throne you who have followed me will also sit upon twelve thrones, judging the twelves tribes of Israel" (v. 28). And in verse 29, Jesus adds, "Every one who has left houses or brothers or sisters or father or mother or children or lands, for my name's sake, will receive a hundredfold, and inherit eternal life."

When we turn to the same passage in the Gospel of Mark, we find the Lord's terminology more precisely recorded. Those who have followed Jesus will in *this time* experience great blessings which will, however, be accompanied by persecutions; but in The Age to Come they will receive eternal life (Mark 10: 30). By comparing these passages, we discover that eternal life, the Kingdom of God, the Kingdom of Heaven, Salvation, The Age to Come all belong together. They are the promise of the future for those who in This Age have become disciples of Christ.

Eternal life belongs to The Age to Come. The Kingdom of God belongs to The Age to Come. If this verse were the only Biblical teaching about eternal life, I would have to conclude that the Kingdom of God will come only when the Lord Jesus returns, and that I shall not inherit eternal life until the day when Christ comes again. Then, I shall enter the Kingdom of God. Then, I shall receive eternal life.

When we pursue this study further we find that the Kingdom of

c

God, like The Age to Come, will follow the resurrection. In I
Corinthians 15: 50, Paul says that "flesh and blood cannot
inherit the kingdom of God." Paul is here speaking about the
resurrection. *Flesh* and *blood* cannot inherit the Kingdom of God.
Our bodies must undergo a transformation so that they no longer
consist of flesh and blood but are incorruptible, glorious, power-
ful, "spiritual" bodies (vv. 42–44). Only in these transformed
resurrection bodies will we enter the Kingdom of God. The
Kingdom of God will come after the resurrection.

In the parable of the tares, we find that the Kingdom of God
will be introduced by the day of judgment. Throughout This
Age, good and evil people—the sons of the Kingdom and the
sons of the evil one—are to live side by side even as wheat and
tares grow together. At the harvest, at "the end of the age"
(Matt. 13: 39) there will be a separation of judgment. "Then shall
the righteous shine forth as the sun in the kingdom of their
Father" (v. 43). Judgment will terminate This Age and bring
the sons of the Kingdom into their full enjoyment of the Kingdom
blessings. In the parable of the net, we find the same structure
with the added fact that judgment will take place at the end of
This Age. "So it will be at the close of the age. The angels will
come out and separate the evil from the righteous, and throw
them into the furnace of fire" (Matt. 13: 49, 50).

Thus we find that the Kingdom of God belongs to The Age
to Come and is set in sharp contrast to This Age. In This Age
there is death; in the Kingdom of God, eternal life. In This Age,
the righteous and the wicked are mixed together; in the Kingdom
of God, all wickedness and sin will be destroyed. For the present,
Satan is viewed as the " god of this age;" but in The Age to Come,
God's Kingdom, God's rule will have destroyed Satan, and
righteousness will displace all evil.

We must therefore modify our diagram of the Ages. This Age
and The Age to Come are not on the same level. This Age is
evil; The Age to Come will witness the fulness of God's Kingdom, the perfection of His reign. Therefore we must place The
Age to Come on a higher level than This Age.[1]

[1] Professor Cullmann's diagram of the New Testament time line does not recognize these two levels of the two ages. This difference was worked out by Geerhardus
Vos in *The Pauline Eschatology* (Grand Rapids: Eerdmans, 1952; originally published
in 1930), p. 38.

The Age to Come

```
                    |————————————————————
          Parousia  |
                    |
                    |
This Age            |
————————————————————
```

When we turn to other passages of Scripture, the transition from This Age to The Age to Come is not as simple as this diagram suggests. Our study thus far suggests that God's redemptive purpose will come to its consummation at the return of Christ at which time the final state of The Age to Come will be ushered in. However, the book of Revelation modifies this structure. After the *Parousia* of Christ (Rev. 19: 11–16) and before The Age to Come (Rev. 21: 1 ff.) is an interval when the saints are raised to reign with Christ for a thousand years (Rev. 20: 1–6). This interval is usually called the Millennium.

The interpretation of this passage raises difficult questions which cannot be here discussed. It is unfortunate that the discussion has often been attended by more heat than light. Some expositors insist that any teaching of a reign of Christ on earth before The Age to Come is Jewish rather than Christian doctrine, while others insist that any non-millenarian eschatology is a departure from loyalty to the Word of God. Such reactions are unfortunate. This question, like others which are, from a practical standpoint, far more important, such as that of the subjects for baptism, should be discussed within the household of faith in a spirit of Christian liberty and charity.

Here, we can only say that it is our conviction that the Scripture teaches that before the final consummation of God's redemptive purpose, the earth is to experience an extended period of our Lord's glorious rule. The church age is the period of Christ's concealed glory; the Age to Come will be the age of the Father's sovereignty when Christ delivers His rule to the Father and becomes Himself subject to the Father (I Cor. 15: 24–28) that God may be all in all. The Millennium will be the period of the manifestation of Christ's glory.[1] If The Age to Come is thought of as existing "beyond history," the Millennium will witness the triumph of God's Kingdom within history.

The problem at the moment is how the New Testament doctrine of the two ages has any room for such an interval. The diagram suggests that The Age to Come begins at the return of Christ and that a millennial reign of Christ can have no place in this prophetic structure.

The solution of this problem is found in what we may call the Biblical prophetic perspective, a phenomenon which occurs throughout the prophetic Scriptures. Usually the prophets, as they looked into the future, spoke of coming events without attempting to give the temporal sequence of the several stages of the accomplishment of God's purpose. Not only is the distant future viewed as a single although complex event, but the immediate future and the distant future are described as though they constituted a single act of God. This is why the Day of the Lord in the prophets is both an historical visitation of God and an eschatological act. It is a Day of judgment when God will disperse Israel in an exile beyond Damascus (Amos 5: 18–27), and it is a Day when God will restore the fortunes of His people (Amos 9: 11 ff.). It is a divine visitation in the form of a plague of locusts and drought (Joel 1: 1–20; see v. 15), and it is the eschatological Day of judgment and salvation (Joel 2: 30–32). The thirteenth chapter of Isaiah reads as though the historical overthrow of Babylon by the Medes would be the end of the world. The historical event is described against the background of the final eschatological drama; both are visitations of the one God in the accomplishment of His redemptive purpose.

This same phenomenon is found in the New Testament. The three accounts of the Olivet Discourse in Matthew 24, Mark 13, and Luke 21 make it clear that our Lord described the historical destruction of Jerusalem by the Romans in A.D. 66–70 against the

[1] See G. E. Ladd, "The Revelation of Christ's Glory," *Christianity Today*, Sept. 1, 1958, pp. 13 f. A somewhat similar line of thought will be found in Oscar Cullmann's essay, "The Kingship of Christ and the Church in the New Testament" in *The Early Church*, edited by A. J. B. Higgins (London: S.C.M. Press, 1956; Philadelphia: Westminster Press, 1956). Professor Cullmann suggests that we should distinguish between the Kingdom of Christ and the Kingdom of God, the former extending through the church age and the Millennium and leading to the latter in The Age to Come (p. 113). This is theologically helpful, but such a terminological distinction cannot be sustained by an exegetical study of the language of the New Testament.

background of the eschatological Antichrist and the Messianic
Woes (the Great Tribulation). The Beast of Revelation 13 is both
actual historical Rome and the future eschatological Antichrist.
In these prophecies, the near and the distant are blended. In such
prophecies as II Peter 3: 12-13, the eschatological events are seen
as a single act of God when the new heavens and the new earth
will emerge out of the judgment of the present order.

From the Old Testament perspective, the church age is not
seen. God is acting in the present for the accomplishment of His
redemptive purpose for Israel, and He will act in the future to
bring His purposes to their consummation when His Kingdom
will fill all the earth. There are indeed prophecies which describe
the coming of a Messianic personage in suffering and humility
such as Isaiah 53 and Zechariah 9: 9-10, other prophecies which
describe a victorious King of the Davidic line (Isaiah 9, 11), as
well as a prophecy of the coming of a heavenly Son of Man in
Daniel 7. But the Old Testament does not relate these several
prophecies to one another, either theologically or chronologically.
God will finally act to redeem His people, and different prophets
describe this eschatological redemption in different terms. The
Old Testament makes no effort to synthesize the prophecies; and
the effort to decide which prophecies apply to the church age,
which apply to the millennial era, and which belong to The Age
to Come ignores this basic fact of the prophetic perspective.

From the New Testament perspective, the eschatological act of
God is usually viewed as a single day which will introduce The
Age to Come. However, the Revelation of John, as well as
I Corinthians 15: 20-28, indicates that there are yet to be two
eschatological stages in the accomplishment of the divine purpose
and the establishment of God's Kingdom. The transition from
This Age to The Age to Come will not occur in a single great
event at the Coming of Christ. We have found that The Age to
Come will be introduced by the resurrection of the dead and the
destruction of the god of This Age. But when we look at the
book of Revelation, chapter 20, we find that there will be two
stages in the resurrection of the dead and two stages in the defeat
of Satan. There is one resurrection at the beginning of the
Millennium (Rev. 20: 4-5) and a second resurrection at its end
(vv. 12-13). Furthermore, we find that there are stages in the

conquest over Satan. At the beginning of the Millennium, Satan is thrown into the abyss and chained for a thousand years (vv. 2–3); but at the end of the Millennium he is released to engage in his nefarious activities again. And even though Christ has ruled over men, Satan finds their unregenerate hearts still responsive to his enticements and ready to rebel against God. Then will occur the last conflict, the final struggle, as a result of which the last judgment will take place when Satan is thrown into the lake of fire. In brief, there are two stages in the defeat of Satan, not just one.

One would never discover this fact from most of the New Testament because it sees the future like a two-dimension canvas in terms of length and breadth without depth. The transition between the ages is viewed as though it were one simple event, even as the Old Testament prophets look forward to a single Day of the Lord. Only when we come to the Revelation do we find Scripture clearly outlining the two stages in the conquest of Satan which are separated by the Millennium. We must therefore modify our diagram again.

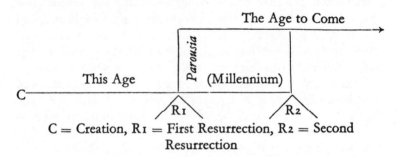

C = Creation, R1 = First Resurrection, R2 = Second Resurrection

We should note one important fact in passing. The Millennium is not the perfect and final manifestation of God's Kingdom. Satan is bound during this period; but when he is released, he finds the hearts of men still responsive to sin. Death and the grave are not destroyed until the final judgment at the end of the Millennium (Rev. 20: 14). We might say, therefore, that the Millennium ends in failure so far as the full achievement of God's reign is concerned. Only in The Age to Come beyond the Millennium is the prayer finally answered, "Thy Kingdom come;

thy will be done on earth as it is in heaven." The earth will then be a renewed earth, to be sure, but it will still be the earth.

Several important conclusions emerge from this study. It is the Biblical teaching that we shall never experience the full blessings of God's Kingdom in This Age. There are those who have identified the Christian hope with a warless world or with a world completely subdued to God's will through the preaching of the Gospel. People who fix their hopes upon a Kingdom which is to be consummated in This Age are certain to be disillusioned. The perfected Kingdom of God belongs to The Age to Come. We shall never know the fulness of its blessings so long as This Evil Age lasts. There will be no world-wide conversion this side of the Coming of Christ. Therefore we ought not to be disillusioned by wars and rumours of wars, by evils and by hostility to the Gospel. And when God's people are called upon to pass through severe sufferings and tribulation, they should remember that God has not abandoned them, but that their sufferings are due to the fact that they no longer belong to This Age and therefore are the object of its hostility.

Furthermore, the Kingdom of God will never be fully realized apart from the personal, glorious, victorious Coming of Christ. Men cannot build the Kingdom of God; Christ will bring it. The powers of Satan and of evil can be finally overcome only by the mighty act of the return of Christ. But that day *is* coming! The Word of God urges us to watch, to be awake, to be ready and waiting for that Day. What assurance, what comfort, what stability it gives to our hearts and minds to know that our prayer will certainly be answered: "Thy Kingdom come, thy will be done on earth, as it is in heaven." Yea, come quickly, Lord Jesus!

CHAPTER III

THE KINGDOM IS TODAY

IN our first two chapters, we have outlined the truth that the Word of God divides the course of God's redemptive purpose into two ages: This Age and The Age to Come. These two ages are separated by the Second Coming of Christ and the resurrection from the dead. The Kingdom of God belongs to The Age to Come and will be realized in its fulness only in that Age. If we had to terminate our study at this point, we would have a redemption which is exclusively one of promise. From this point of view, salvation would be only an insurance policy. To be sure, insurance is very important; but it is only a protection for the future against the day of trouble. It has no value to me today except to give me a sense of security. If all we had were this single division between the ages at the return of Christ, salvation would be only the promise of deliverance in the Day of Judgment. Indeed, the promise of eternal life in Mark 10 belongs altogether to the future when the Kingdom of God comes.

However, we have discovered that the transition from This Age to The Age to Come will not occur at a single point. We found there was an overlapping between This Age and The Age to Come. There is not a single resurrection of the dead, but two resurrections which are separated by the Millennium. There are two stages in the defeat of Satan. At the beginning of the Millennium he will be bound and thrown into the abyss. At the end of the Millennium, he will be loosed, only to be cast finally into the lake of fire for ever. There is to be an overlapping of these two ages during the millennial period. The earth will enjoy a new measure of the life and blessings of the Kingdom of God before the final consummation in The Age to Come. God's reign, His rule, will express itself in two great acts, one before and one after the Millennium.

If this were the complete programme of redemption, we would have merely a religion of promise, a gospel of hope. The fact is, however, there is a further overlapping of the two ages. There are a number of explicit statements in the New Testament, as well as the basic structure of New Testament theology as a whole, which compel us to conclude that the blessings of The Age to Come remain no longer exclusively in the future but have become objects of present experience in This Age.[1] Hebrews 6: 5 speaks of those who "tasted . . . the powers of the age to come." The Age to Come is still future, but we may taste the powers of that Age. Something has happened by virtue of which that which belongs to the future has become present. The powers of The Age to Come have penetrated This Age. While we still live in the present evil Age and while Satan is still the god of This Age, we may taste the powers of The Coming Age. Now a taste is not a seven-course banquet. We still look forward to the glorious consummation and fulfilment of that which we have only tasted. Yet a taste is real. It is more than promise; it is realization; it is experience. "Taste and see that the Lord is good." We have "tasted the powers of The Age to Come."

Again in Galatians 1: 4, we read that Christ "gave himself for our sins to deliver us from the present evil age." How can men and women who live in an evil age be delivered from its power? This deliverance comes from the power of The Age to Come which has reached back and projected itself in the person of Christ into the present evil Age so that we, by the power of The Age to Come, may be delivered from this present evil Age.

The same truth is set forth in Romans 12: 2: "Do not be conformed to this age but be transformed by the renewal of your mind, that you may prove what is the good and acceptable and perfect will of God." How can we live in the midst of the evil Age and not be conformed to it? We are to experience an inner transformation which is itself the result of the power of The Age to Come reaching back into this present evil Age. While the evil Age goes on, God has made it possible for us to experience a new power that we might thereby prove what is God's will. This

[1] See the study by the present author in *The Expository Times* 68 (1957), pp. 268–273.

overlapping of the two ages is fundamental to our understanding of the Biblical teaching of redemption.

Such sayings lead to the conclusion that there is not only a future overlapping of the ages in the millennial period but also a present overlapping of The Age to Come and This Age, and that we are now living "between the times." We are in fact caught up in the conflict of the ages. This may be illustrated by a further modification of our diagram.

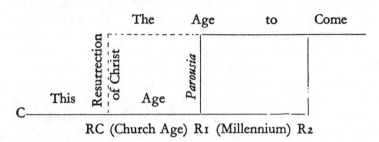

RC (Church Age) R1 (Millennium) R2

What does this have to do with the Kingdom of God? Just this: the Kingdom of God belongs to The Age to Come. Yet The Age to Come has overlapped with This Age. We may taste its powers and thereby be delivered from This Age and no longer live in conformity to it. This new transforming power is the power of The Age to Come; it is indeed the power of the Kingdom of God. The Kingdom of God is future, but it is not only future. Like the powers of The Age to Come, the Kingdom of God has invaded this evil Age that men may know something of its blessings even while the evil Age goes on.

Perhaps the most important scripture expounding the fundamental character of the Kingdom of God is I Cor. 15: 22-26. "For as in Adam all die, so also in Christ shall all be made alive. But each in his own order: Christ the firstfruits, then at his coming those who belong to Christ. Then comes the end, when he delivers the kingdom to God the Father after destroying every rule and every authority and power. For he must reign until he has put all his enemies under his feet. The last enemy to be destroyed is death."

In this passage Paul is describing the various stages by which God will accomplish His redemptive purpose. This purpose has to do with the Kingdom of God. The ultimate objective is the accomplishment of God's Kingdom, *i.e.*, the realization of God's perfect reign in all the universe. This is accomplished by the defeat of His enemies. Christ must reign until He has put all His enemies under His feet. When these enemies are at last subdued, Christ will hand over the Kingdom to God. The Kingdom of God therefore is the reign of God through Christ destroying the enemies of God's reign.

The conquest of the Kingdom, according to this passage, finds its highest expression in the defeat of death. "The last enemy to be destroyed is death" (v. 26). God will manifest His mighty power as the sovereign over all things by the final destruction of the awful enemy of all God's creatures: death.

However, this conquest of God's reign is not accomplished in a single great act. Paul speaks of three stages in the triumph of divine power. Let us translate verse 23 literally: "Christ the first-fruits; *after that* they that are Christ's at his coming. *After that* comes the end, when he delivers up the kingdom to God." We have already seen that the book of Revelation divides the resurrection into two stages which it calls the first and (supposedly) the second resurrection. Paul shows us that there are in fact three stages in this triumph of divine power, and that the resurrection of Jesus Christ is in fact the "firstfruits" or the first act of the first resurrection itself. *The resurrection* began with the resurrection of Christ. At His *Parousia* will occur the resurrection of those who belong to Christ. This is not a "general" resurrection but a resurrection only of those who have shared the life of Christ, *i.e.*, Christian believers. Only "after that" comes the end when Christ gives the Kingdom to the Father. Since this third stage will witness the final conquest of death, the "last enemy," we must conclude that Paul looked forward to a resurrection of "the rest of the dead" similar to that pictured in Revelation 20: 12 ff. We have therefore three stages in the conquest over death: the final resurrection, the "first" resurrection, and the firstfruits of the first resurrection in the resurrection of Christ. This may be indicated in our diagram by the symbols RC, R_1, R_2.

Here is something that is utterly thrilling. The resurrection of our Lord Jesus is the beginning of the final resurrection. How do I know there will one day be a resurrection of the dead when we are to be raised in the likeness of Christ? What is my assurance of that hope? The answer is a fact in history: the resurrection already has begun. This is the significance of Jesus' words, "Because I live, you will live also" (John 14: 19). This is the meaning of the power of His resurrection (Phil. 3: 10) and the resurrection life which we may now share (Eph. 2: 5). Christ's resurrection is not an isolated event; it is in fact an eschatological occurrence which has been transplanted into the midst of history. We are living already on the heavenward side of the first stage of the resurrection. This puts a new light on the whole human predicament. Heaven has already begun in that the resurrection has already begun to take place. "Christ the firstfruits, then they that are Christ's at his *Parousia*. Then comes the end."

This conquest of death in the three stages of the resurrection is a threefold manifestation of the Kingdom of God. The last two stages agree with the outline we have already discovered in the Revelation of John. "Then (after his coming) comes the end, when he delivers up the Kingdom to God" (v. 24). This corresponds to Rev. 20: 10 and 14: "and the devil who had deceived them was thrown into the lake of fire and brimstone. . . . Then Death and Hades (the grave) were thrown into the lake of fire." At the end of the millennial reign of Christ, the last enemy, death, will be destroyed. This is the final result of Christ's kingly reign. Then, Christ will deliver up the Kingdom to God the Father, for by His reign He has subdued all His enemies.

A previous stage of this conquest occurs at the beginning of the Millennium. This is stated both in Rev. 20: 4 as well as in I Cor. 15: 23, "Then they that are Christ's at his coming."

This is what the Kingdom of God means: the defeat of the enemies of God. The Kingdom of God means the reign of our Lord Jesus Christ until all His enemies are put under His feet. And who are His enemies? Wicked men? Antichrist? Godless nations? We have already found our point of departure in the Scripture. "The last enemy to be destroyed is death." Paul defines the Kingdom of God in terms of the conquest of such enemies as death.

Whence comes death? The Word of God is clear. "The wages of sin is death" (Rom. 6: 23). Death comes because of sin.

The *last* enemy to be destroyed is death; therefore sin is also an enemy and sin must likewise be destroyed.

Whence comes sin? What is the source of evil? It is of course Satan. Here we have a hellish triumvirate—a trinity from the pit —Satan, sin, death. "He must reign until He has put all his enemies under His feet." This is the triumph of God's King dom.

We have seen from our diagram and from our earlier studies that the defeat of Satan is to be accomplished in at least two stages. At the end of the Millennium he is thrown into the lake of fire for ever. But at the beginning of the Millennium he is shut in the abyss and chained for a thousand years. And now we come to the crucial question of this chapter: Has anything yet been accomplished in the triumph of Christ over His enemies? Or is our salvation altogether a matter of promise? Does the defeat of sin, Satan, death through the reign of Christ belong exclusively to the future, or is there an initial victory which has been accomplished?

The answer to this important question has already been suggested from our study of I Cor. 15. The conquest over death is in *three* stages, and the first of them has already been accomplished. God's Kingdom—the activity of God's kingly power through Christ—has already manifested itself in history in Christ's resurrection. The triumph over death has begun.

Now we must ask the next question: Is the defeat over sin and Satan altogether future? Or has God already acted in His kingly power to break the power of Satan? In other words, has the Kingdom of God invaded the present evil Age—the domain of Satan?

Let us take our point of departure again from an important verse in the Word of God. Hebrews 2: 14: "Since therefore the children (that is, those whom God would make His children) share in flesh and blood (*i.e.*, since we are human beings), he (Christ) himself likewise partook of the same nature, that through death He might destroy him that has the power of death, that is, the devil, and deliver all those who through fear of death were subject to lifelong bondage." This is a verse which many have never read accurately. There are many who tell us that the defeat of Satan will occur only with the *Parousia* of Christ in glory. They read this verse as though it said, "that through his *Parousia* he might destroy him who has the power of death, that is the devil." But no! It is through His death that Christ has destroyed Satan.

We must admit that this is a perplexing verse. How can it be that Satan has been destroyed? The perplexity is caused by our English translations. The Greek word here used has no adequate equivalent in English. "Destroy" means "to ruin" or "to annihilate completely." The Greek word, *katargeo*, literally means "to put out of action," "to render inoperative." This "destruction" of Satan was accomplished by Christ's death. Christ in death did something which was a defeat for the devil in that his activity, his power, was in some real way curtailed.

Now we have these *three* stages in the defeat of Satan: at the end of the Millennium, the lake of fire; at the beginning of the Millennium, the abyss; and at the Cross the initial defeat. As the Kingdom of God manifests itself in three stages in the conquest of death, so the Kingdom of God also reveals its power in three stages in the defeat of Satan.

We find this same truth of the present conquest of evil in the Gospels. In Matthew 4: 23-24, we read of the beginning of our Lord's ministry, "And he went about all Galilee, teaching in their synagogues and preaching the gospel of the kingdom and healing every disease and every infirmity among the people. So his fame spread throughout all Syria, and they brought him all the sick, those afflicted with various diseases and pains, demoniacs, epileptics, and paralytics, and he healed them."

"Preaching the gospel of the kingdom," "healing every disease": is there any connexion between these two phrases? Is there any relationship between the Good News about the Kingdom of God and our Lord's healing ministry?

We may find the answer in the first recorded miracle in Mark's Gospel. Jesus came to Capernaum and on the Sabbath day He entered into a synagogue and began to teach. People were astonished at His teaching for He taught them as having authority and not as the scribes. "And immediately there was in their synagogue a man with an unclean spirit; and he cried out, 'What have you to do with us, Jesus of Nazareth? Have you come to destroy us? I know who you are, the Holy One of God.' But Jesus rebuked him, saying, 'Be silent, and come out of him!' And the unclean spirit . . . came out of him. And they were all amazed, so that they questioned among themselves, saying, 'What is this? A new teaching!'" What was new about it? The Gospel of the Kingdom. What was the novel element? "With authority he commands even the unclean spirits, and they obey him" (Mark 1: 23–27). Our Lord's ministry and announcement of the Good News of the Kingdom were characterized by healing, and most notably by the casting out of demons. He proclaimed the Good News of the Kingdom of God, and He demonstrated the Good News of the Kingdom of God by delivering men from the bondage of Satan.

The twelfth chapter of Matthew clearly sets forth the exorcism of demons as the work of God's Kingdom. Opposition to our Lord had become intense, but the Pharisees were dumbfounded by Jesus' mighty power. They had to give some explanation of His mighty works, and so they said, "It is only by Beelzebub, the prince of demons, that this man casts out demons" (Matt. 12: 24). The Pharisees recognized the presence of supernatural power; but they attributed it to the activity of the Devil himself. "Knowing their thoughts, he said to them, 'Every kingdom divided against itself is laid waste, and no city or house divided against itself will stand; and if Satan casts out Satan, he is divided against himself; how then will his kingdom stand?'" (vv. 25–26). It is ridiculous to say that Satan is casting out Satan. That would be civil war, internal strife; that cannot be. What is the explanation of Jesus' power? "But if it is by the Spirit of God that I cast out demons, then the kingdom of God has come upon you" (v. 28).

What is the Gospel of the Kingdom? What means the announcement that the Kingdom of God has come near? It is this: that God is now acting among men to deliver them from bondage to Satan. It is the announcement that God, in the person of Christ, is doing something—if you please, is attacking the very kingdom of Satan himself. The exorcism of demons is proof that the Kingdom of God has come among men and is at work among them. The casting out of demons is itself a work of the Kingdom of God.

Let us change the idiom and go back to the structure of the

two ages. Jesus' power over demons was the disclosure that the powers of The Age to Come have invaded the present evil Age. It was the proof that the Kingdom of God, which belongs to the age of the future when Christ comes in glory, has already penetrated This Age. Satan is not yet destroyed as he will be when he is cast into the lake of fire. Satan is not yet bound as he will be during the Millennium in the abyss. Yet God's Kingdom is active; God is attacking the kingdom of Satan. "If it is by the Spirit of God that I cast out demons, then the kingdom of God has come upon you" (v. 28). The casting out of demons is accomplished by the power of God's Kingdom. The exorcism of demons is proof that the Kingdom of God is present.

Now let us look carefully at verse 29. "Or how can one enter a strong man's house and plunder his goods, unless he first binds the strong man? Then indeed he may plunder his house." This is one of the most important verses in the New Testament for an understanding of the Kingdom of God. Satan is "the strong man" and "his house" is This Age. The strong man's goods are demon-possessed men and women. The question is, How can anyone enter into Satan's realm and deprive him of his goods except he *first* bind the strong man? Then shall he spoil his goods.

Now may we ask the all-important question: Is Satan bound? Is there some sense in which our Lord in His incarnation and earthly ministry has bound the Evil One?

At first thought this may seem impossible, for the Word of God says Satan goes about like a roaring lion seeking whom he may devour. However, we must ask what this teaching of the binding of Satan really means. We must remember that Satan is not a creature of flesh and blood but a being in the spirit world. What kind of a chain will one use to bind an angel, a spirit? What sort of bond will hold him? Will a rope do? Is a strait-jacket adequate? Is iron strong enough, or forged steel, or perhaps titanium? It is obvious that the teaching of the binding of Satan is a metaphor. A metaphor is a truth, but it is not a literal, *i.e.,* physical, truth, because a literal chain or a literal rope cannot bind a spiritual being. The binding of Satan means that the coming of Christ, His presence on earth, the exercise of His power among men, has accomplished a defeat of Satan so that his power is broken. Satan *is* bound.

There is no necessity to identify this verse with Rev. 20: 2 where it says that Satan was taken and bound with a strong chain and cast into the abyss for a thousand years. These two verses refer to two entirely different events. Those who hold a non-millennial interpretation usually identify these two passages. This identification, however, is unlikely. Yet Matt. 12: 28 clearly says that the Kingdom of God has entered into the present evil Age. The power of Satan has been broken because in some sense Satan has been bound and men and women may now be delivered from bondage to satanic power. Satan is a defeated enemy; and because of the work of Christ I may be delivered from the power of darkness and brought into the Kingdom of God's dear Son.

This same truth of the defeat of Satan through the earthly ministry of our Lord is set forth in the tenth chapter of Luke. The Lord had sent seventy disciples on a preaching tour just before His final journey to Jerusalem. In His instructions for their mission, He said, "Heal the sick . . . and say to them, 'The Kingdom of God has come near to you'" (Luke 10: 9). In the person of our Lord's emissaries, the Kingdom of God came to the cities they visited. And what if they were not received? "But whenever you enter a town and they do not receive you, go into its streets and say, 'Even the dust of your town that clings to our feet, we wipe off against you; nevertheless know this, that the kingdom of God has come near.' I tell you, it shall be more tolerable on that day for Sodom than for that town. Woe to you, Chorazin! Woe to you, Bethsaida! for if the mighty works done in you had been done in Tyre and Sidon, they would have repented long ago, sitting in sackcloth and in ashes. But it shall be more tolerable in the judgment for Tyre and Sidon than for you" (vv. 10–14).

Why did our Lord pronounce such a fearful judgment on these cities? Because the Kingdom of God had come to them. The evidence of the presence of the Kingdom of God was the healing of the sick. The signs of the Kingdom were manifest; its power was at work in cities like Chorazin and Bethsaida. Rejection of the disciples and their mission meant rejection of the Kingdom of God, and this could result only in fearful judgment.

"The seventy returned with joy, saying, 'Lord, even the demons are subject unto us in your name!'" (v. 17). "We

D

healed the sick; yes, and as we went out announcing that the Kingdom of God has come near, even the demons were subject to us, and we cast them out." "And he said to them, 'I saw Satan fall like lightning from heaven.'" (v. 18). "While you were preaching the Kingdom and casting out demons, I was watching Satan fall from heaven. In your ministry of delivering men and women from bondage of Satan, I saw his fall." Are we to try to construct some kind of cosmological drama from this verse and imagine that Satan who was "up there" is now "down here"? I do not think so. Rather, this verse means that Satan has been thrust down from the pinnacle of his power. This is the same truth we have found in Matt. 12: 28. Satan has been bound; Satan has fallen like lightning from heaven. His power has come tumbling down. And here is the evidence: "The Kingdom of God has come upon you"; demons are cast out, men and women are delivered from the power of Satan that they may enter into the power and the life and the blessing of the Kingdom of God.

God's Kingdom means the divine conquest over His enemies, a conquest which is to be accomplished in three stages; and the first victory has already occurred. The power of the Kingdom of God has invaded the realm of Satan—the present evil Age. The activity of this power to deliver men from satanic rule was evidenced in the exorcism of demons. Thereby, Satan was bound; he was cast down from his position of power; his power was "destroyed." The blessings of the Messianic Age are now available to those who embrace the Kingdom of God. We may already enjoy the blessings resulting from this initial defeat of Satan. Yes, the Kingdom of God has come near, it is already present.

This does not mean that we now enjoy the *fulness* of God's blessings, or that *all* that is meant by the Kingdom of God has come to us. As we said in the previous chapter, the Second Coming of Christ is absolutely essential for the fulfilment and consummation of God's redemptive work. Yet God has already accomplished the first great stage in His work of redemption. Satan is the god of This Age, yet the power of Satan has been broken that men may know the rule of God in their lives. The evil Age goes on, yet the powers of the Age to Come have been made available to men. To the human eye, the world appears

little changed; the kingdom of Satan is unshaken. Yet the Kingdom of God has come among men; and those who receive it will
be prepared to enter into the Kingdom of Glory when Christ
comes to finish the good work He has already begun. This is the
Gospel of the Kingdom.

CHAPTER IV

THE MYSTERY OF THE KINGDOM

THE fourth chapter of Mark and the thirteenth chapter of Matthew contain a group of parables which set forth the "mystery of the kingdom of God" (Mark 4: 11). A parable is a story drawn from the everyday experience of the people which is designed to illustrate the central truth of our Lord's message. This central truth is called "the mystery" of the Kingdom.

We must first establish the meaning of the term "mystery." A mystery in the Biblical sense is not something mysterious, nor deep, dark, profound and difficult. In modern English, the word may bear such connotations, but we cannot interpret the Bible by modern English. In Scripture, "mystery" is often a technical concept whose meaning is set forth in Romans 16: 25–26. Paul writes, "Now to him who is able to strengthen you according to my gospel and the preaching of Jesus Christ, according to the revelation of the mystery which was kept secret for long ages but is now disclosed and through the prophetic writings is made known to all nations." Here is the Biblical idea of mystery: something which has been kept secret through times eternal but is now disclosed. It is a divine purpose which God has designed from eternity but has kept hidden from men. At last, however, in the course of His redemptive plan, God reveals this purpose, and by the Scriptures of the prophets makes it known to all men. A mystery is a divine purpose, hidden in the counsels of God for long ages but finally disclosed in a new revelation of God's redemptive work.

The parables set forth the mystery of the Kingdom—a new truth about the Kingdom of God which was not revealed in the Old Testament but which is at last disclosed in the earthly ministry of our Lord. What is this mystery?

To answer this question, we must go back into the Old Testament and look at a typical prophecy of the coming of God's Kingdom. In the second chapter of Daniel, King Nebuchadnezzar was given a vision of a great image which had a head of gold, a chest of silver, thighs of bronze, legs of iron, and feet of iron and clay. Then he saw a stone, cut out without hands, which smote the image on the feet and ground it to powder. This dust was swept away by the wind "so that not a trace of them could be found." Then the stone which destroyed the image became a great mountain which filled the whole earth (Dan. 2: 31–35).

The interpretation is given to us in verses 44 and 45. The image represents the successive nations which were to dominate the course of world history. The meaning of the stone is given in these words: "And in the days of those kings the God of heaven will set up a kingdom which shall never be destroyed, nor shall its sovereignty be left to another people. It shall break in pieces all these kingdoms and bring them to an end, and it shall stand forever; just as you saw that a stone was cut from a mountain by no human hand, and that it broke in pieces the iron, the bronze, the clay, the silver, and the gold. A great God has made known to the king what shall be hereafter."

Here is the Old Testament perspective of the prophetic future. The Prophets look forward to a glorious day when God's Kingdom will come, when God will set up His reign on the earth. You will remember that we have discovered that the basic meaning of the Kingdom of God is God's reign. In that day when God sets up HIS reign, it will displace all other reigns, all other kingdoms and authorities. It will break the proud sovereignty of man manifested in the rule of the nations which have dominated the scene of the earthly history. God's reign, God's Kingdom, God's rule will sweep away every opposing rule. God alone will be King in those days.

In the Old Testament perspective, the coming of God's Kingdom is viewed as a single great event: a mighty manifestation of God's power which would sweep away the wicked kingdoms of human sovereignty and would fill all the earth with righteousness.

We must now turn back to the Gospel of Matthew and relate this truth to our previous study. John the Baptist had announced the coming of the Kingdom of God (Matt. 3: 2) by which he understood the coming of the Kingdom foretold in the Old Testament. The Coming One would bring a twofold baptism: Some would be baptized with the Holy Spirit and experience the Messianic salvation of the Kingdom of God, while others would be baptized with the fires of the final judgment (Matt. 3: 11). That this is John's meaning is clear from the next verse. Messiah's work will be one of sifting and the separation of men. As the farmer threshes and winnows his harvest, preserving the good grain and discarding the chaff, Messiah will cleanse his threshing floor, gathering the grain into his barn (salvation for the righteous) but sending the wicked into the fiery judgment (v. 12). The phrase "unquenchable fire" shows that this refers to no ordinary human experience but to the eschatological judgment.

From his prison, John sent messengers to Jesus to ask if He really was the Coming One, or if they were to look for another. John's doubt has often been interpreted as a loss of confidence in his own mission and divine call because of his imprisonment. However, Jesus' praise of John makes this unlikely. John was no reed shaken by the wind (Matt. 11: 7).

John's problem was created by the fact that Jesus was not acting like the Messiah whom John had announced. Where was the baptism of the Spirit? Where was the judgment of the wicked?

Jesus replied that He was indeed the Bearer of the Kingdom, that the signs of the Messianic Age of prophecy were being manifested. And yet Jesus said, "Blessed is he who takes no offence at me" (Matt. 11: 6). "Lord, are you He who is to come, or shall we look for another?" Why did John ask that question? Because the prophecy of Daniel did not seem to be in process of fulfilment. Herod Antipas ruled in Galilee. Roman legions marched through Jerusalem. Authority rested in the hands of a a pagan Roman, Pilate. Idolatrous, polytheist, immoral Rome ruled the world with an iron hand. Although Rome exercised great wisdom and restraint in governing her subjects, granting to the Jews concessions because of their religious scruples, yet only God possessed the right to rule His people. Sovereignty belongs to God alone. Here was John's problem; and it was the problem of every devout Jew, including Jesus' closest disciples, in their effort to understand and interpret Jesus' person and ministry. How could He be the bearer of the Kingdom while sin and sinful institutions remained unpunished?

Jesus answered, "Blessed is he who takes no offence at me." What Jesus meant is this. "Yes, the Kingdom of God is here. But there is a mystery—a new revelation about the Kingdom. The Kingdom of God is here; but instead of destroying human sovereignty, it has attacked the sovereignty of Satan. The Kingdom of God is here; but instead of making changes in the external, political order of things, it is making changes in the spiritual order and in the lives of men and women."

This is the mystery of the Kingdom, the truth which God now discloses for the first time in redemptive history. God's Kingdom is to work among men in two different stages. The Kingdom *is* yet to come in the form prophesied by Daniel when every human sovereignty will be displaced by God's sovereignty. The world will yet behold the coming of God's Kingdom with power. But the mystery, the new revelation, is that this very Kingdom of God has now come to work among men but in an utterly unexpected way. It is not now destroying human rule; it is not now abolishing sin from the earth; it is not now bringing the baptism of fire that John had announced. It has come quietly, unobtrusively, secretly. It can work among men and never be recognized by the crowds. In the spiritual realm, the Kingdom now offers to men the blessings of God's rule, delivering them from the power of Satan and sin. The Kingdom of God is an offer, a gift which may be accepted or rejected. The Kingdom is now here with persuasion rather than with power.

Each of the parables in Matthew 13 illustrates this mystery of the Kingdom, that the Kingdom of God which is yet to come in power and great glory is actually present among men in advance in an unexpected form to bring to men in the present evil Age the blessings of The Age to Come.

The first parable of Matthew 13 is that of the four kinds of soil. The sower went out to sow. As he scattered the seed, some fell upon the path that ran through the field. This seed did not take root but, lying exposed, was soon picked up by the birds. Other seed fell on rocky ground where the earth was shallow because a ledge of rock lay under the thin earth. This seed soon sprouted and started to grow; but when the hot, burning weather came, the ground quickly dried out and the sprouts died, for there was not enough depth of soil to hold moisture in hot weather. Still other seed fell in thorny places. The seed sprouted, but the thorns also sprang up and choked the growth so that it did not mature. Some seed fell upon soft, deep, clean ground where it was able to mature and ripen and produce a harvest.

The mystery of the Kingdom is this: The Kingdom of God is here but not with irresistible power. The Kingdom of God has come, but it is not like a stone grinding an image to powder. It is not now destroying wickedness. On the contrary, it is like a man sowing seed. It does not force itself upon men. Some, like the good soil, receive it; but there are many others who do not receive it. Some hear the word of the Kingdom but it never enters their heart. They hear the Gospel of the Kingdom but they do not understand the truth which they hear. Satan comes and snatches away the seed. There is no root, there is no life.

Others are shallow. They hear the Word of the Kingdom; they seem to receive it; they make a response. There is the semblance of life, but there is no depth. Perhaps the intellect or the emotions have been stirred but the will has not been moved. There is no real life. When trouble arises, when they find that the reception of the Gospel of the Kingdom does not deliver them from evil; indeed, when they meet persecution and evil for the very reason that they have received the message of the Kingdom, they wither and die because there is no life. Their profession is spurious.

Still others are like the thorny ground. They seem to receive the word of the Kingdom, they appear to believe and to evidence life. But they are not prepared to accept the humble form of God's Kingdom. The care of the age, the love of riches, the ambition, the ostentation, the pressure of conformity to This Age in which they still live choke the Word and it becomes unfruitful.

This is the mystery of the Kingdom: that the Kingdom of God has come among men and yet *men can reject it*. The Kingdom will not experience uniform success. Not all will receive it. This was a staggering thing to one who knew only the Old Testament. When God's Kingdom comes, it will come with *power*. Who can resist it? Who can withstand God? But precisely this is the mystery of the Kingdom. The Kingdom is here, but it can be rejected. One day God will indeed manifest His mighty power to purge the earth of wickedness, sin and evil; but not now. God's Kingdom is working among men, but God will not compel them to bow before it. They must receive it; the response must come from a willing heart and a submissive will.

God is still dealing with us in this same way. God will not drive you into His Kingdom. It is not the business of those who are called to the ministry of the Word to speak with authoritarian compulsion. We speak as emissaries of God, but we plead and do not demand, we persuade and do not drive. We implore men to open their hearts that the Word of His Kingdom may have its fruitage in their lives. But man can reject it. They can spurn the Gospel of the Kingdom. They can scorn the preacher of the Word; and he is helpless.

The parable of the tares or weeds illustrates another facet of this same truth. A man sowed wheat in his field but his enemy sowed weeds. When the weeds were discovered the servants wanted to pull them out, but they were told to let both wheat and weeds grow until the harvest. Then the separation would take place. Until harvest time, weeds and wheat must grow together.

It is of utmost importance to note that "the field is the world" (v. 38). Where do we get the notion that the field is the Church? Jesus Himself said that the field is the world, not the Church. It is a misinterpretation of the Word of God to say that the parable teaches that in the Church the good and the bad, the regenerate and the unregenerate, are to grow together until the harvest and that we cannot exercise church discipline since it would disrupt the order of things. Our Lord said no such thing. He was not talking about the mixed character of the Church but about the world.

Furthermore, we read that "the good seed means the sons of the kingdom; the weeds are the sons of the evil one, . . . the harvest is the close of the age" (vv. 38–39). At the end of This Age, the angels will come and separate the wheat from the weeds.

There is to be a sure day of judgment bringing a final separation between the righteous and the wicked.

What is the point of this parable? In the book of Daniel when God's Kingdom comes, it will destroy sinners and sweep all wickedness and iniquity from the face of the earth. In this parable, Jesus says that the Kingdom of God has come already and is already at work in the world; but it is not destroying sin, it is not purging the earth of evil. The Kingdom of God is indeed here but in a different way from that which had ever been anticipated. The sons of the Kingdom—those who have received the Gospel of the Kingdom—and the sons of the evil one are to live together *in the world* until the end of the age. Only then will there occur the final separation. To one who knew only the Old Testament, this was an amazing announcement. When God's Kingdom comes, the wicked will be no more. But Jesus taught, "The Kingdom has come; it is here working among you. Yet wicked men still continue to live in your midst. The Kingdom has come, but the evil Age goes on. The Kingdom has come, but the wicked and the righteous must live together in a mixed society until the coming of the Son of Man."

The unforseen character of the coming of the Kingdom among men is further illustrated in the third and fourth parables of the mustard seed and the leaven. In ancient Semitic idiom, the mustard seed was a proverbial symbol for that which is tiny and insignificant. The mustard was a plant which rapidly grew into a very large shrub. Jesus said, "The kingdom of heaven is like a grain of mustard seed which a man took and sowed in his field; it is the smallest of all seeds, but when it has grown, it is the greatest of shrubs and becomes a tree, so that the birds of the air come and make nests in its branches" (Matt. 13: 31–32).

This parable illustrates that the Kingdom of God is present among men but in a form not previously revealed. It is here as something tiny, as something insignificant, as something as small as a mustard seed. The important thing is that even though it is like a tiny seed, it is still the Kingdom of God. Jesus says, "Do not let its apparent insignificance deceive you. Do not be discouraged. The time will come when this same Kingdom of God, which now is here like the tiny seed, will be a great shrub, so great that the birds of the heaven will come and lodge in its branches."

The message of this parable is not the way in which the tiny seed becomes a tree. Many interpreters have placed great emphasis upon the element of growth and have used it to illustrate the gradual extension of the Church in the world. This is not the point of the parable. If our Lord had wished to teach slow growth and gradual expansion, the illustration of the mustard seed which quickly becomes a large shrub would not serve this purpose. The slow growth of the oak would have been far more suitable to illustrate the gradual growth of the Kingdom. Growth is not the truth in this parable. It has nothing to teach us about *how* the Kingdom will come in the future. We know from other Scriptures that the Kingdom of God will come in mighty power. It will possess the earth only when the Lord Himself returns in majesty and glory. The form of this future coming is not an element in this parable. One truth is set forth: the Kingdom of God which one day shall fill the earth is here among men but in a form which was never before expected. It is like an insignificant seed of mustard. This tiny thing *is*, however, God's Kingdom and is therefore not to be despised.

The parable of the leaven illustrates the same truth. "The kingdom of heaven is like leaven which a woman took and hid in three measures of meal, till it was all leavened" (Matt. 13: 33). The Hebrew housewife could not buy a yeast cake at the corner grocery. She had to take a piece of dough that already was leavened and put it in a batch of unleavened dough.

This parable is often interpreted in one of two directions. Many have taken it as a basic proof-text that the Gospel is destined to conquer all the earth by gradual influence. These interpreters emphasize that the way leaven works is by gradual, slow permeation and penetration. Others insist that leaven always symbolizes evil and that the parable teaches the apostasy of the Church.

At this point, we must turn aside for a moment to emphasize an all-important characteristic of parables. In the parabolic method of teaching, we are not to look for truth in every detail. A parable is a story drawn from the familiar experiences of everyday life, and many of the details of the parable are simply elements of local colour. A parable is not a fabricated story. An allegory is a story created from the imagination and therefore capable of being so fashioned by its creator that every detail can convey some aspect of the truth being illustrated. A parable is not an allegory. Instead of a story fashioned by its author, it is an incident drawn from daily experience which necessarily contains details which do not convey spiritual truth and which therefore are not to be pressed in the interpretation.

This principle deserves illustration, for it is essential to avoid misinterpretation of the Kingdom parables. Jesus told a story of a man going down from Jerusalem to Jericho which is called the parable of the Good Samaritan (Luke 10: 30–37). This story could have happened any day of the week. The parable answers one question: "Who is my neighbour?" (v. 29). Most of the details are merely picturesque background. Who is the traveller? Any man. What is Jerusalem? What is Jericho? Any two cities in the world. The questions become more difficult when we ask, Who are the robbers? How many were there? What spiritual truth is suggested by the donkey? What spiritual truth is represented by the coins which the Samaritan paid to the innkeeper? Why two coins? Who is the innkeeper? What does the hotel represent? What spiritual truth is embodied in the oil and wine? Where did the Samaritan go after leaving the inn? It is obvious that most of those details belong simply to the local colour of the parable.

This principle is even clearer in the parable of the unrighteous steward (Luke 16: 1–13). Here is a parable from Jesus' lips involving dishonesty. If we must find meaning in the details in the story, we must admit that Jesus taught that the end justifies the means. Dishonesty, sharp practice, is not wrong if good comes from it! This obviously is not what our Lord taught. A single truth is set forth in this parable: Men should be wise in the use of their substance. They should invest it so that it will help them in the day of (spiritual) need (v. 9). All else is local colour.

This principle is essential in understanding the parable of the leaven. The truth is not that of the gradual permeation of the world by the Kingdom. Scripture nowhere else teaches this. The truth is the same as that of the mustard seed. In its present manifestation, the Kingdom of God is like a handful of leaven in a big bowl of dough. The dough swallows up the leaven so that one is hardly aware of its presence. It is almost unobservable; it can scarcely be seen. Instead of the glory of God shaking the earth, the Kingdom has come in One who is meek and lowly, who is destined to be put to death, who has only a handful of disciples. Little wonder that Roman historians hardly mention the career of Jesus. From the world's point of view, His person and mission could be ignored. But one should not be deceived thereby; some day the whole earth will be filled with God's Kingdom even as the leavened dough fills the entire bowl. The means by which this end is accomplished is no element of the parable.

The other faulty interpretation is that leaven is a symbol of evil and that the parable pictures the professing Church which is to be so permeated by evil in the last days that the whole Church will become apostate and corrupted from a pure faith. It is indeed a fact that frequently, perhaps even in most places where leaven is used in Scripture, it is a symbol of evil. But this is not always true. The most important place where leaven was used in Biblical history was at the time of the Exodus. The Israelites were commanded to eat unleavened bread on this occasion but not because leaven was a symbol of evil and unleavened bread of purity. Exodus 12: 39 says, "And they baked unleavened cakes of the dough which they brought out of Egypt, for it was not leavened, because they were thrust out of Egypt and *could not tarry.*" Leaven is not here a symbol of evil; but unleavened bread was a symbol of *haste.* The Israelites could not take time for the leaven to work.

Again, in Leviticus 23, leavened bread was *commanded* in the celebration of the feast of Pentecost. At this feast, Israelites were to bring two loaves of leavened bread as a sacrifice to God. The feast of Pentecost was the feast of harvest, a time of rejoicing. An offering of thanksgiving was presented to God because He had granted the harvest. The sacrifice consisted of two loaves of ordinary leavened bread such as was used in the household, representing the firstfruits of the grain harvest. In the observance of this festival, the use of leaven was commanded of God's people as a symbol of rejoicing and thanksgiving. To see in this feast a type of the apostate church is uncontrolled allegorizing.

The parable of leaven involves no symbolism of evil. The interpretation that leaven is evil is faced with the problem of explaining how the true Kingdom of God, the realm of salvation, as well as the Kingdom in its so-called "mystery form" of the professing church, can become thoroughly permeated by evil. This parable is related in Luke 13: 20–21 where it has no relationship to the outward Davidic kingdom but to the spiritual kingdom. Leaven does not here refer to evil. It illustrates the truth that the Kingdom of God may sometimes seem to be a small, insignificant thing. The world may despise and ignore it. What could a Galilean carpenter and a dozen Jews accomplish? But do not be dismayed, the day will come when God's Kingdom will fill all the earth even as the leaven fills the whole bowl. God's purposes will not be frustrated.

The parables of the treasure and the costly pearl (Matt. 13: 44–46) logically follow those of the mustard seed and the leaven. The Kingdom of God is like a tiny seed of mustard, a tiny bit of leaven; but even though its form is insignificant, it *is* the Kingdom of God. Therefore it is of inestimable value. Even though it has come among men in a humble form, our Lord says that the Kingdom of heaven is like a treasure whose value transcends every other possession; it is like a pearl whose acquisition merits the loss of all other goods. Now again, the idea that this man *buys* the field or that the merchant *buys* the pearl has nothing to do with the basic truth of the parable. This parable does not tell us that we can buy salvation. Salvation is by faith, the free gift of God; and Matt. 20: 1–16 teaches that the Kingdom is a gift and not a reward which can be earned. Yet even though the Kingdom is a gracious gift, it is also costly. It may cost one his earthly possessions (Mark 10: 21), or his friends or the affections of his family or even his very life (Luke 14: 26). But cost what it may, the Kingdom of God is like a treasure or a costly pearl whose possession merits any cost.

The parable of the draw-net reaffirms the truth that though the Kingdom of God has come among men now in an unexpected manner, it will nevertheless issue in the final judgment and in the separation of the good from the wicked and the destruction of evil. The revelation of the coming of the Kingdom in the Old Testament emphasized this catastrophic, apocalyptic event. When

God brings His Kingdom, the society of wicked men will be displaced by the society of those who have submitted themselves to God's rule who will then enjoy the fulness of the divine blessings freed from all evil. Jesus taught that the redemptive purposes of God had brought His Kingdom to work among men in advance of the day of judgment. It is now like a drag-net which gathers within its influence men of various sorts, both good and bad. The separation between the good and the evil is not yet; the day of judgment belongs to the end of the age (Matt. 13: 49). Meanwhile, there will be within the circle of those who are caught up by the activity of God's Kingdom in the world not only those who are truly sons of the Kingdom; evil men will also be found in this movement.

The parable of the wheat and the weeds describes the character of the world at large; the good and the evil are to live side by side until the day of judgment. The structure of human society is not to be at this time disrupted by the final separation of men. The parable of the drag-net has a narrower reference and describes the circle of men who are influenced by the activity of God's Kingdom in the person of Christ. Evil men will find their way into that fellowship. This explains how there could be a Judas in the immediate circle of our Lord's disciples. It explains how perverse men can arise within the bosom of the Church (Acts 20: 29-30) who will turn men away from Christ. It helps us to understand how a modern church, however careful it may be in its efforts to preserve a Biblical purity of membership, will nevertheless find people in its midst who turn out to be alien to the interests of God's Kingdom.

We should include in this study of the mystery of the Kingdom an important parable found only in the Gospel of Mark. The Kingdom of God is "as if a man should scatter seed upon the ground, and should sleep and rise night and day, and the seed should sprout and grow, he knows not how. The earth produces of itself, first the blade, then the ear, then the full grain in the ear. But when the grain is ripe, at once he puts in the sickle, because the harvest has come" (Mark 4: 26-29). This parable is similar to that of the mustard seed in that the element of growth is not the point of the story. The modern mind, coloured by an evolutionary point of view, sees in the idea of growth the concept of gradualness and slow development. This, however, is a modern and not a Biblical idea. Paul can use the metaphor of growth to illustrate that which is utterly supernatural—the resurrection of the dead (I Cor. 15: 36–38).

The parable of the seed growing by itself sets forth a single basic truth: "the earth beareth fruit of itself." The Kingdom of God is like a seed in this one point: a seed contains the principle of life within itself. There is nothing the farmer can add to the life in the seed. He cannot make it grow, he cannot cause it to produce life. His one task is to sow the seed. Then he may go about his other tasks. But while he is busy about other things, even while he is asleep, the life resident within the seed and the powers resident in the earth assert themselves and produce fruit.

The Kingdom of God is a miracle. It is the act of God. It is supernatural. Men cannot build the Kingdom, they cannot erect it. The Kingdom is the Kingdom of *God*; it is God's reign, God's rule. God has entrusted the Gospel of the Kingdom to men. It is our responsibility to proclaim the Good News about the Kingdom. But the actual working of the Kingdom is God's working. The fruitage is produced not by human effort or skill but by the life of the Kingdom itself. It is God's deed.

This is the mystery of the Kingdom: Before the day of harvest, before the end of the age, God has entered into history in the person of Christ to work among men, to bring to them the life and blessings of His Kingdom. It comes humbly, unobtrusively. It comes to men as a Galilean carpenter went throughout the cities of Palestine preaching the Gospel of the Kingdom, delivering men from their bondage to the Devil. It comes to men as his disciples went throughout Galilean villages with the same message. It comes to men today as disciples of Jesus still take the Gospel of the Kingdom into all the world. It comes quietly, humbly, without fire from heaven, without a blaze of glory, without a rending of the mountains or a cleaving of the skies. It comes like seed sown in the earth. It can be rejected by hard hearts, it can be choked out, its life may sometimes seem to wither and die. But it *is* the Kingdom of God. It brings the miracle of the divine life among men. It introduces them into the blessings of the divine rule. It is to them the supernatural work of God's grace. And this same Kingdom, this same supernatural power of God will yet manifest itself at the end of the age, this time not quietly within the lives of those who receive it, but in power and great glory purging all sin and evil from the earth. Such is the Gospel of the Kingdom.

CHAPTER V

THE LIFE OF THE KINGDOM

JESUS said to Nicodemus, "Unless one is born again, he cannot see the kingdom of God," and "Unless one is born of water and the Spirit, he cannot enter the kingdom of God" (John 3: 3, 5). These verses associate the Kingdom of God with eternal life. They indicate that one must enter into life in order to enter into the Kingdom of God; he must be born again.

There is a great hunger in the human heart for life. A person must be abnormal or emotionally unbalanced to surrender the love for life. A university professor had been plagued for years by an endocrine deficiency which had caused life to weigh so heavily upon him that he finally despaired, swallowed poison and snuffed out life. The burden of suffering and weariness had become so heavy that this intelligent man's perspective had become distorted and warped. It is natural for man to love life and to cling to it.

God's Word offers a life higher than the physical life which all men enjoy. It is the life of the Kingdom of God. We are all familiar with this text, "Unless one is born again, he cannot see the kingdom of God." But frequently we dissociate eternal life from the truth of the Kingdom of God and do not usually think of eternal life as an aspect of God's Kingdom. However, these verses join together these two great Biblical realities. They are in fact inseparable. The life which Christ came to bring us is the life of God's Kingdom.

In the previous chapter we have expounded the Biblical teaching about the Mystery of the Kingdom. This Mystery is a new disclosure of the divine purpose which had not been revealed to the Old Testament saints. From the perspective of the Old Testament revelation the coming of the Kingdom of God was expected to bring a transformation of the existing order. God's

Kingdom would change the political order and displace all human rule and authority (Isa. 2: 1–4).

We must now add a further Biblical truth: When the Kingdom of God comes, it will effect also a transformation of the very physical order (Isa. 11: 6–9). The earth is to be transformed. There is to be new heavens and a new earth. The creation is to be delivered from bondage to decay and corruption (Isa. 65: 17; 66: 22).

The Mystery of the Kingdom is this: that the Kingdom which will one day change the entire external order has entered into This Age in advance to bring the blessings of God's Kingdom to men and women without transforming the old order. The old age is going on, yet men may already enjoy the powers of The Age to Come. The kingdom of Satan still stands, but the Kingdom of God has invaded the kingdom of Satan. Men and women may now be delivered from this power, delivered from this bondage, delivered from the mastery of sin and death. This deliverance is accomplished because the power of the future Kingdom of glory has come among men in a secret, quiet form to work in their midst.

I have retraced these steps by way of introduction because this same structure is embodied in the Biblical truth of eternal life. Eternal life belongs to the future Kingdom of glory and to The Age to Come; yet this eternal life has become available to man in the present evil Age.

In Matthew 25 we find a prophetic portrait of the separation of the nations by the judgment of the Son of Man. He will judge men as sheep are separated from goats. The result of this separation is announced in verse 34, "Then the King will say to those at his right hand, 'Come, O blessed of my Father, inherit the kingdom prepared for you from the foundation of the world.'" If this were the only verse we had about the Kingdom of God, we would have to conclude that it is altogether future, that the Kingdom of God will not come until Christ returns, that there is to be a final judgment of men when the righteous will be introduced into the blessings of God's Kingdom.

But consider carefully verse 46. This verse summarizes the entire passage. "And they"—the wicked—"will go away into eternal punishment, but the righteous into eternal life." The righteous will inherit the Kingdom; that means that they will go away into *eternal life*. The Kingdom of God which will be established when Christ comes again and eternal life are here synonymous. Eternal life then belongs to the future. Eternal life belongs to the Kingdom which Christ will establish by His appearing in glory.

The same truth is found in Matthew 19. We have already studied this chapter in another context. A young man came to Jesus and said, "Teacher, what good deed must I do to have eternal life?" (v. 16). This is the same eternal life of which we have just read in Matthew 25: 46. Jesus replied in effect: "You must cut yourself loose from all other loyalties and follow me." Thereupon the young man turned away. He would not pay the price. Then Jesus said to His disciples, "Truly, I say to you, it will be hard for a rich man to enter the kingdom of heaven" (v. 23). "But, Lord, we thought this young man asked the way to *eternal life*; and you say, It is hard for a rich man to enter the kingdom of heaven. Are the kingdom of heaven and eternal life the same thing?" So it appears. The young man might as well have asked how he could enter into the Kingdom of God, and Jesus could have answered, "It is hard for a rich man to inherit eternal life."

Jesus added, "Again I tell you, it is easier for a camel to go through the eye of a needle than for a rich man to enter the kingdom of God" (v. 24). When the disciples heard it, they were astonished and said, "Who then can be saved?"

Eternal life—the Kingdom of God—the Kingdom of heaven— salvation; all of them belonging to the future, all of them reserved for the disciples of the Lord Jesus.

If this were the entirety of the Gospel, I would have to conclude that I cannot now enjoy eternal life. Salvation, eternal life await us in the future. Some day, we shall be saved. Perhaps we could say that we are saved today in the sense that we are confident that some day we shall enter into eternal life. But salvation in this sense is only the guarantee that when Christ comes, *then* we shall enter into the Kingdom, *then* we shall enter into eternal life. If these verses constituted the totality of the Gospel, we could enjoy no experience of eternal life here and now. Life would belong exclusively to the future, to the glorious Kingdom of God. How can eternal life be both a future blessing and at the same time a present reality?

Life does indeed belong to the future. Paul makes this clear in his discussion of the resurrection in II Corinthians 5. He looks forward to a day when we shall receive "a building from God, a house not made with hands" (v. 1). This hope will be fulfilled at the Coming of Christ when the saints will put on resurrection bodies. In our present mortal bodies, we "sigh with anxiety" (v. 4) and long for a different body. Death is a repelling experience for it suggests departure from the body—"nakedness." What Paul longs for is not to be "unclothed"—disembodied—but to be "clothed upon," *i.e.,* to put on the resurrection body, "that what is mortal may be swallowed up by life" (v. 4).

This is eternal life. Eternal life has to do with the total man. It concerns not only my soul but also my body. When we finally inherit the Kingdom of God (I Cor. 15: 50), that which is mortal —our physical, frail body—will be swallowed up in life. Eternal life includes the redemption of our bodies. The inheritance of the Kingdom of God means the transformation of these bodies of flesh and blood (I Cor. 15: 50). All of us, even though we have received the gift of life, are dying. With some, the descent to the grave will be a long, gradual, painful one. With others, it occurs with shocking suddenness. Some will enjoy a large measure of vigour until the very end. But we are all on our way to the grave, for we are dying, mortal creatures.

God has something better for us. There will come a day when that which is mortal shall be swallowed up in life. The backaches, headaches, jangled nerves, arthritis, strained hearts, ulcers and cancers will all be healed in the influx of the life of The Age to Come. Our doctors, dentists and surgeons will have no more patients. Our hospitals, sanatoriums and institutions will be empty. Eternal life will mean the salvation, the transformation of the body.

The futurity of eternal life is again taught in the Revelation. John writes, "Then he showed me the river of the water of life, bright as crystal, flowing from the throne of God and of the Lamb through the middle of the street of the city; also, on either side of the river, the tree of life with its twelve kinds of fruit, yielding its fruit each month; and the leaves of the tree were for the healing of the nations" (Rev. 22: 1–2). This is a beautiful promise of the full realization of life. The river of the water of life: we shall drink of it and die no more. The tree of life: we shall eat of its fruit, and the frailty, the decay, the suffering, the misery and the dying will all disappear. Then we shall experience the full meaning of the life which God has for us. The leaves of the tree of life are for the healing of the nations. Shall we make a liniment of these leaves and rub it on our pains, or shall we make a brew and drink it? To ask such questions indicates that this is a picture, it is poetry; but it is a poetical representation of a glorious, objective fact. Mortality will be swallowed up in life.

John goes on: "There shall no more be anything accursed, but the throne of God and of the Lamb shall be in it, and his servants shall worship him" (v. 3). Here is the greater reality. Wonderful as is the salvation of the body, the greater reality is that God will dwell in the very midst of His people. "They shall see his face" (v. 4). Barriers of the flesh and sin will be swept away. We shall see His face. Here is perfection of fellowship, full enjoyment of God's love. "And his name shall be on their foreheads" (v. 4). Here again is a symbolic way of saying that God will perfectly possess His people and enjoy untroubled fellowship. We shall perfectly belong to Him, and God's purposes will be completely fulfilled within us. This is life; this is life eternal; this is the life of the Kingdom of God.

This is proved by Paul's words in the resurrection chapter, where we read in I Cor. 15: 24–26, "Then comes the end, when he delivers the kingdom to God the Father. . . . For he must reign until he has put all his enemies under his feet. The last enemy to be destroyed is death." Then, He will restore the Kingdom to the Father. Then, eternal life will reign, for death will be destroyed. Then, the Kingdom of God will be all in all, for its enemies are no more. This is the eternal life of God's Kingdom. It is not merely a life which relates to our spirits; it has to do with the whole man. God cares for our bodies; He has purposed to redeem them.

Life is future. And yet, in the Gospel of John, we find such a statement as this: "I came that they may have life, and may have it abundantly" (John 10: 10). Jesus came to give us life today—

THE LIFE OF THE KINGDOM
not only in the future at the end of the age, but now. Somehow the life of The Age to Come has come to us here and now while we are still in our mortal bodies living in the evil Age.

This truth is reiterated, "He who believes in the Son has eternal life" (John 3: 36). "He who hears my word and believes him who sent me, has eternal life; he does not come into judgment, but has passed from death to life" (John 5: 24). We *have* everlasting life; it is our possession now. In its fulness? Hardly. An aeroplane plummets to the ground destroying all its human cargo. Christian and pagan—believer and unbeliever—both die. We are not preserved, we are not removed from the ravages of sickness and suffering and death. Yet the Word of God says, "He who believes in the Son has everlasting life." How can this life be both future and present?

In these verses about eternal life we find the same structure which we have discovered in our study of the two ages and the Kingdom of God. The Age to Come belongs to the future, and yet the powers of The Age to Come have entered into the present evil Age. The Kingdom of God belongs to the future, and yet the blessings of the Kingdom of God have entered into the present Age to deliver men from bondage to Satan and sin. Eternal life belongs to the Kingdom of God, to The Age to Come; but it, too, has entered into the present evil Age that men may experience eternal life in the midst of death and decay. We enter into this experience of life by the new birth, by being born again.

What is this eternal life? Of what does this blessing consist? First, eternal life means the knowledge of God. "And this is eternal life, that they know thee the only true God, and Jesus Christ whom thou hast sent" (John 17: 3).

The Biblical idea of knowledge is not simply the apprehension of facts by the mind. That is a Greek idea. Knowledge in the Bible is far more than intellectual apprehension. Knowledge means experience. Knowledge means personal relationship. Knowledge means fellowship. I *know* my friend John. That does not mean that I have read a sketch about him in *Who's Who* and can recite some facts as to his place of birth, his age, his wife, children, profession, etc. I could recite all these facts and yet not know him. I could know much about him and still not know the man. To know a person means that I have entered into fellowship with him, that I have a relationship with him, that we have shared each other in the mutuality of friendship.

This is life eternal, not that you may be able to recite a creed, or quote some Bible verses, or recite some facts about God. That is not knowledge of God. "This is eternal life, that they know thee the only true God." Fellowship with God; friendship with God; personal relationship to God: this is life eternal.

Let us go back to the book of Revelation: "The throne of God and of the Lamb shall be in it, and his servants shall worship him; they shall see his face, and his name shall be on their foreheads" (Rev. 22: 3–4). In The Age to Come, the life of that glorious Kingdom means perfection of our fellowship with God and of our knowledge of God. We shall see Him face to face.

Life eternal means that we have *already* been brought into a personal relationship with God here and now. Life eternal means that we have already been introduced to God. Life eternal means that God has become our God and we have become His people, and that we have begun to share a fellowship with Him; we have begun to share His life.

This knowledge of God properly belongs to The Age to Come, to the day when the Kingdom will finally be established. This is made clear in Jeremiah's prophecy (31: 31–33) of the day when God's Kingdom comes in power and glory. "Behold, the days are coming, says the Lord, when I will make a new covenant with the house of Israel and the house of Judah, not like the covenant which I made with their fathers when I took them by the hand to bring them out of the land of Egypt. . . . But this is the covenant which I will make with the house of Israel after those days, says the Lord: I will put my law within them, and I will write it upon their hearts, and I will be their God, and they shall be my people." Note particularly the next verse: "And no longer shall each man teach his neighbour and each his brother, saying, 'Know the Lord,' for they shall all know me, from the least of them to the greatest, says the Lord." In that day there will be no more Bible conferences, no Bible Schools and Seminaries, no Sunday Schools and classes of instruction, for all will know the Lord and will need instruction no longer.

Here is a picture of a consummated fellowship when men have entered into a personal, profound, perfect knowledge of God.

But this knowledge of God properly belongs to The Age to Come, to that day when God's will is perfectly consummated upon the earth. That is the vision of Jeremiah 31. It is this intimate, direct knowledge of God which constitutes eternal life.

But the teaching of our Lord in the Gospel of John is that already we have entered into eternal life; already we have been introduced into this knowledge of God. Somehow, the future has become present. The blessing of The Age to Come has been made available to men now. Not in its fulness and perfection, to be sure: yet the knowledge of God in John 17: 3 is not promise; it is realization, present experience, a present fellowship which will be wonderfully enlarged and perfected in The Age to Come.

This knowledge of God includes an apprehension of God's truth, not merely in the intellectual realm but in the impact of truth upon life. Knowledge of the truth includes the intellectual element but it does not stop there. Thus Scripture speaks of "doing the truth" (John 3: 21). When we attain to a perfect knowledge of God, we shall also enjoy an apprehension of God's truth which we do not now possess. Then we shall not have Presbyterians and Baptists, Calvinists and Arminians, premillennialists and amillennialists and postmillennialists, but we shall all understand perfectly what the truth of God is, for we shall be taught of God.

God has permitted us to attain something of the knowledge of divine truth here and now; yet at best, it is partial and incomplete. Nevertheless, it is real. Although imperfect, it is the greatest and most wonderful reality in life, because the truth of God brings men into fellowship with God.

The partial character of this knowledge creates practical problems. It will indeed be a wonderful day when all of God's people can agree in their understanding of God and of God's truth. That day lies in the future; it is not yet here. Many problems arise because God's people do not recognize the teaching of Scripture about the incompleteness of Christian knowledge. Sometimes, people insist that there ought to be a complete conformity in all details of understanding of God and of Christian doctrine which is not warranted by the Word of God. The Scripture is clear that our knowledge is partial. It is because of the very imperfectness of our knowledge, says Paul in I Corinthians 13, that we must exercise the gift of love. The various ministrations of the Holy Spirit in the early Church in prophecy, tongues, knowledge (supernatural disclosures of divine truth) were given to men because now we know in part (I Cor. 13: 12). They belong to our "childhood," *i.e.*, to our earthly life. When we attain perfect maturity, when we see face to face and know fully even as also we were fully known (I Cor. 13: 11–12), we shall put away childish things. We shall no longer need these aids of the Holy Spirit to help fill in our ignorance. However, when other gifts have passed away, love abides. Love is that gift of the Spirit, above all others, which will characterize our perfected fellowship in The Age to Come. This love we now enjoy, and the Church on earth will be a colony of heaven, enjoying in advance the life of The Age to Come *to that extent* to which we permit the Holy Spirit to manifest the gift of love in our mutual relationships, especially in those areas where our imperfect knowledge leads to differing interpretations of the Word of God in the details of theology.

Paul clearly asserts this fact in I Cor. 13: 12. Now in This Age, "we see in a mirror, dimly." The ancient mirror was a piece of polished metal which tarnished and pitted easily. It gave an imperfect image. One could recognize the reflection, but it was far from perfect. Now, in This Age, we see in a mirror, imperfectly; "but then face to face." In The Age to Come, we shall no longer see a reflected likeness, we shall see face to face.

Now look carefully at the last part of verse 12. "Now I know in part." There is no man who ever lived, apart from the Lord Jesus Himself, who can say, "I am the truth. You must follow me!" The inspired Apostle said, "Now I know in part." This puts us all in a place of humility before God. We must search the Scriptures, we must study God's Word, we must wait on God. But because we are still in the evil Age, when we have done our best, we are compelled to say, "Lord, I have searched Thy Word; but I know only in part; I do not perfectly understand."

"Now I know in part." This lays a demand upon us that we hold the Word of God both in humility and in charity: in humility towards God and in charity towards our brethren. One day, we shall see face to face and shall know even as we are known by God. But what a precious thing it is to be permitted to enjoy the fundamental verities of this knowledge of God before we attain to The Age to Come. "This is eternal life, that they know thee."

The second meaning of eternal life is the life of God's Spirit dwelling within us. "Except a man be born again, . . . except a man be born of water and the Spirit, he cannot see, . . . he cannot enter the kingdom of God." The life of The Age to Come is the work of the Spirit of God. In I Corinthians 15, Paul looks forward to the life of The Age to Come, the life of the Kingdom of glory, the life when these mortal bodies will be transformed; and he describes this life with the words, "It is sown in corruption, it is raised in incorruption; it is sown in dishonour, it is raised in glory; it is sown in weakness, it is raised in power; it is sown a natural body, it is raised a spiritual body" (I Cor. 15: 42-44, A.V.).

What is a *spiritual* body? At first thought the very phrase might seem to involve a contradiction in terms. How can one talk of a spiritual body? A body is material, and spirit is the opposite of matter. It is true that the ancients sometimes conceived of spirit in terms of very fine matter, but such is not Paul's thought. A "spiritual body" is not a body which consists of spirit. It is rather a body whose life, whose energy is derived from Spirit—God's Spirit. A spiritual body is therefore a real body, a tangible, objective body, but one which is completely and perfectly energized and animated and empowered by the Holy Spirit of God.

We have already met this essential thought in II Corinthians 5 where Paul is looking forward to the day when mortality is swallowed up in eternal life (v. 4). Now look carefully at verse 5: "Now he that hath wrought us for the selfsame thing is God, who also hath given us the earnest of the Spirit" (A.V.). And in Ephesians 1: 13-14, Paul says, "In him you also, who have heard the word of truth, the gospel of your salvation, and have believed in him, were sealed with the promised Holy Spirit, which is the guarantee of our inheritance until we acquire possession of it." What is this inheritance? It is the fulness of life, the redemption of the body, the transformation of our mortal frame into the fulness of the strength and power and glory of a "spiritual body." This inheritance is in view in all three passages: I Corinthians 15: 42-50; II Corinthians 5: 1-10, and Ephesians 1: 14. But we do not yet have possession of this inheritance. However, we have more than a promise; God has given unto us the Holy Spirit as an *earnest* (A.V.) or a *guarantee* (R.S.V.).

What is an earnest? We do not use this word frequently in everyday conversation, but we have a different word to express the same idea. An earnest is a down-payment. It is far more than a "guarantee," as R.S.V. translates it, it is partial but actual possession. If you decide to buy a house, you search until you find the house you want. Perhaps it costs twenty thousand dollars; the price is a bit high, but it is the house for which you have been looking. Thereupon you promise the owner that on an appointed day you will deliver the money, and you sign a bill of sale. Does that give you a claim upon the house? It does not. Suppose you say, "Let us go down to the notary public, and I will put myself under oath that on such and such a date, I will pay for the house." Will that give you a claim on the house? It will not. Suppose you bring a group of friends as character witnesses who testify what an honest, honourable fellow you are and what a good bank account you have. Will that give you a claim on the house? It will not. There is one thing that will bind the agreement: Money! Cash! Not $20,000, not the entire cost of the house, but a substantial down-payment. This is "earnest money."

The present possession of the Holy Spirit is a down-payment. It is more than promise although it *is* promise. It is more than guarantee although it *is* a guarantee. It is the present although partial possession which guarantees the full possession at the proper time. This is the life of the Spirit, eternal life. The fulness of life awaits the Coming of Christ; but until the mortal is swallowed up in life, God has given us His Spirit as a down-payment. The indwelling of the Spirit is the down-payment of that life which we shall one day experience in its fulness. The new birth is the beginning, partial but real, of the life of The Age to Come. This means that already we have within us the life of heaven. It means we already participate in the life that belongs to God's future Kingdom; not indeed in its fulness, but nevertheless in reality.

Let us look at one more phrase which describes this same truth in different terms. In Romans 8: 22–23 Paul is describing the future redemption of the whole creation in The Age to Come, the day when God's redemptive purpose will be completed and the creation will be delivered from the bondage of corruption into the glorious liberty of the sons of God. "We know that the whole creation has been groaning in travail together until now; and not only the creation, but we ourselves, who have the first-fruits of the Spirit, we groan inwardly as we wait for adoption as sons, the redemption of our bodies." Here we have the same wonderful truth again. Some day our very bodies are to be redeemed. Some day the whole physical creation is to be transformed. Some day the life which flows from Christ's resurrection will renovate the whole structure of human existence. Until that day, what? We groan: we are burdened. We have pain. We suffer. We die. But not only so: we have the *firstfruits of the Spirit*.

What are firstfruits? Let me illustrate firstfruits by some fruit trees in my garden. In the late winter, I prune the trees and spray them. When spring comes, the blossoms break out and I know the trees are alive. But blossoms are not firstfruits. They are promise, for if there were no blossoms there would certainly be no fruit; but I have seen trees loaded with blossoms which never produced fruit. After the blossoms the leaves break out, but there is as yet no fruit. Soon after the leaves the little hard green fruit sets. Is this the firstfruits? One year, one tree was loaded with small hard plums, but later there came a wind storm which blew them all off the tree. I had a peck of small green plums on the ground, but I had no harvest. This is not the firstfruits.

Firstfruits come when the fruit has begun to ripen. You watch the tree day by day. Then comes the day when that first peach is at last ripe. You have been waiting for that day and you pick off that luscious peach, the first peach of the season, the only one on the tree which is quite edible. All the rest are a little green, too hard to be eaten. But here is one peach. You sink your teeth into it and the juice titillates your taste buds, and you revel in the flavour of the first peach. That is the firstfruits. It is not the harvest, but it is the *beginning of the harvest*. It is more than promise; it is experience. It is reality. It is possession.

God has given us His Spirit as the firstfruits of the life to come in the resurrection. When Christ comes, we will receive the harvest—the fulness of life from God's Spirit. But God has already given to us His Spirit as a firstfruits, a foretaste, an initial experience of that future heavenly life.

Has the realization gripped you that the very life of heaven itself dwells within you here and now? Did you ever know that? I am afraid we live most of our life in terms of promise. We often sing of the future, and so we ought to sing. Our Gospel is a Gospel of glorious promise and hope. Yes, the best, the glorious best, is yet to be. And yet we are not to live alone for the future. The future has already begun. The Age to Come has reached into This Age; the Kingdom of God has come unto you. The eternal life which belongs to tomorrow is here today. The fellowship which we shall know when we see Him face to face is already ours, in part but in reality. The transforming life of the Spirit of God which will one day transform our bodies has come to indwell us and to transform our characters and personalities.

This is what eternal life means. This is what it means to be saved. It means to go about every day in the present evil Age living the life of heaven. It means that every local fellowship of God's people who have shared this life should live together and worship and serve together as those who enjoy a foretaste of heaven here on earth. This is what the fellowship of a Christian Church ought to be. May God help us to live the life of The Age to Come in the midst of an evil Age. God has already brought us into fellowship with Himself. This is the promise, the down-payment, the earnest, the Holy Spirit dwelling in us, the life of The Age to Come. This is the Gospel of the Kingdom. This is the life of The Age to Come.

CHAPTER VI

THE RIGHTEOUSNESS OF THE KINGDOM

IN the Sermon on the Mount our Lord describes the righteousness of the Kingdom. The importance of this Kingdom righteousness is found in Matthew 5: 20, "For I tell you, unless your righteousness exceeds that of the scribes and Pharisees, you will never enter the kingdom of heaven." The Sermon on the Mount outlines the conditions of entrance into the Kingdom of Heaven. This verse links together the future and the present aspects of the Kingdom. The qualification for entrance into the future Kingdom is a present righteousness, a righteousness which exceeds that of the Scribes and Pharisees. What kind of righteousness is this?

The righteousness required for entrance into the future realm of God's Kingdom is the righteousness which results from God's reign in our lives. The Kingdom of God gives to us that which it demands; otherwise, we could not attain it. The righteousness which God requires is the righteousness of God's Kingdom which God imparts as He comes to rule within our lives.

In our text the righteousness now demanded is set in contrast with the righteousness of the Scribes and the Pharisees. This is significant because the Scribes and Pharisees were profoundly interested in righteousness. The Scribes were the professional students of religion. They were the men who gave their full time, like professors in a theological seminary, to the study of the Scriptures and whose main objective was the definition of righteousness. The Pharisees were those who accepted the teachings of the Scribes—their disciples who put their teachings into practice, thereby aiming to achieve a life of righteousness.

The Scribes and their disciples were motivated by the sole concern of achieving righteousness. Yet our Lord says that His disciples must possess a righteousness which exceeds that of the Pharisees. How can this be done? The Scribes had developed an enormous body of law to define what was right and what was wrong. They devoted more attention and study to the definition of righteousness than any of us do.

For instance, the law says that men should not work on the Sabbath Day. If righteousness consists of obedience to law, the law must be explicit. The question then arises, "What is work?" If conformity to the will of God is defined in terms of law, then one must know precisely when he is obeying the law and when he is breaking it. The Scribes and the Pharisees did not leave anything to private judgment or to the leading of the Holy Spirit. They wanted a definition of what was right and what was wrong in every possible situation. Therefore they had compiled a great mass of tradition providing this necessary definition of righteousness which became embodied in the Mishnah and later still in the Talmuds.

What is work? Let me illustrate the problem. As I come home from worship on the Sabbath I see a dead leaf on a rose bush beside my walk. I stop and pick off the dead leaf. Have I worked? Probably not. Then I see a dead twig and I break off the twig. Have I yet engaged in work? Then I see another branch which I cannot break off, so I take my pocket-knife and I cut it off. Have I broken the Sabbath? There is still another branch as big as my thumb, too large for my knife, so I get my clippers and snip it off. Have I worked yet? The final step is to prune all my roses.

If I am living in terms of law, I must have a dictum from God's law that I may know when I am within the will of God, because my salvation depends upon it. I must know what is work and what is not.

Here is an actual illustration from Jewish rabbinic lore. A man keeps chickens. On the Sabbath one of his chickens lays an egg. Is it right to eat the egg or is it wrong? Is work involved or not? To the Scribes, this was a serious problem and the Rabbis debated the question and came to the following decision. If a man kept chickens for the purpose of producing eggs and they laid eggs on the Sabbath, work was involved and to eat the egg meant to break the Sabbath. But if he kept chickens for some other purpose and they happened to lay eggs on the Sabbath, no work was involved; the eggs could be eaten without breaking the

Sabbath. This may seem humourous to us; but from the viewpoint of the orthodox Jew whose salvation depended upon keeping the law, the terms of his salvation were no laughing matter.

Jesus said, "Unless your righteousness exceeds that of the Scribes and Pharisees, you will never enter the kingdom of heaven." What is the greater righteousness of the Kingdom? The answer is found in the specific illustrations of righteousness given by our Lord, which embody a number of principles or "laws."

First, we have the Law of Anger. "You have heard that it was said to the men of old, 'You shall not kill; and whoever kills shall be liable to judgment'" (Matt. 5: 21). Old Testament law, the rabbinic tradition, and modern law recognize that there are different kinds of homicide. Deliberate murder is not the same as accidental homicide; and while both result in the death of an innocent victim, there is a difference in motivation of the action and therefore a difference in degree of guilt which the law takes into account.

Jesus went much further. "I say unto you, that every one who is angry with his brother shall be in danger of the judgment; and whosoever shall say to his brother, Raca, shall be in danger of the council; and whosoever shall say, Thou fool, shall be in danger of the hell of fire" (Matt. 5: 22, R.V.). The King James Version completely changes the meaning of the saying by translating: "Whosoever is angry with his brother *without a cause*." The translation of the Revised Version says, "Anger is sin"; that of the King James Version says, "Unjustified anger is sin." The explanation of this divergence is simple. If you read these words in the oldest Greek Bibles in existence, you would not find the words "without a cause." These words are not in the text but were inserted by copyists because the language of our Lord seemed to be too radical. Who can avoid becoming angry once in a while? Surely the Lord couldn't have meant that all anger condemns men to perdition. He must have had reference to unjustifiable anger, anger for which there is no provocation. The apparently harsh saying of the oldest Greek texts was softened by the addition of a single Greek word, *eike*, translated in our King James Version, "without a cause." However, this is not what our

F

Lord said. "Whoever is angry with his brother shall be in danger of the judgment." This is the reading of our oldest Greek Bibles which were not known by the translators of the Authorized Version.

"Whosoever shall say to his brother, Raca, shall be in danger of the council," *i.e.,* shall be liable to trial and condemnation before the court. "*Raca*" is an Aramaic word which may mean "Empty head!" but we do not know enough about the Aramaic tongue to be sure of its meaning. In any case, it is a word of strong emotion, an expression of anger; and this is all that is necessary for our understanding.

"Whosoever shall say, Thou fool, shall be in danger of the hell of fire." When I was a boy, I was very careful never to call anyone a "poor fool," even in jest, because I had read this verse. I was certain that if my tongue slipped and I happened to call someone a fool, I would be sure to go to hell. This is not quite the way this verse is to be taken, for again, we do not know precisely what the Aramaic word means. But the real meaning of our Lord's words is not found in the precise significance of "*raca*" and "fool." The point is that both words, and many others, are evidence of anger and contempt towards another; and it is this anger with which our Lord is here concerned, whatever form of expression it takes.

What did Jesus mean? Is anger as bad as murder? Is the hurling of an evil epithet at another which wounds his spirit as serious a sin as the hurling of an axe which spills his brains? This cannot be our Lord's meaning, else we wreck the moral code. What Jesus meant was this: "Murder is sin, indeed; but I say unto you, Anger is sin." Here is the root of the matter: Anger is sin. Have you ever found yourself in a situation where you were deeply angry; and while you did not murder anyone, if you had given vent to your feelings you could have done so. If looks could split a man's skull, someone's head would have been laid open from ear to ear. Where there is such anger in your heart, where there is an evil attitude towards another, there is sin. Murder is anger full-grown.

The scribal teaching laid the emphasis upon the outward act. A man might harbour hatred towards another but not be guilty of serious sin if he restrained his anger. Jesus says, This is not true righteousness. It is not the outward act which is the all-important thing but the attitude of a man's heart. If down in the heart there is smouldering hatred and bitter anger which is expressed in nothing more deadly than words or even thoughts, in the sight of God one is a sinner and deserving hell. You may never have swung a club or thrown a stone or thrust a knife; but if the heart harbours bitterness, hatred, anger, Jesus said that you are condemned before God as a sinner.

The righteousness which the Kingdom of God demands is not concerned alone with outward acts of sin. It goes behind the act, behind the deed, to the heart, and deals with what a man is in himself before God. Kingdom righteousness says, What you *are* is more important than what you *do*. Except your righteousness exceeds the righteousness of the Scribes and Pharisees, you will never enter the Kingdom of God.

Kingdom righteousness demands that I have no evil in my heart towards my fellow man. It is obvious that such a heart righteousness can itself be only the gift of God. God must give what He demands. If we know the righteousness of the Kingdom of God, the anger and the animosity which frequently rises within us because we are fallen human beings can be transformed into an attitude of love and concern. The righteousness of God's Kingdom is the product of God's reign in the human heart. God must reign in our lives now if we are to enter the Kingdom tomorrow.

We have next the Law of Purity. "You have heard that it was said, 'You shall not commit adultery.' But I say to you that every one who looks at a woman lustfully has already committed adultery with her in his heart" (vv. 27–28). Again, the greater righteousness of the Kingdom of God is a righteousness of the heart in contrast to mere rightness of conduct. The scribal law forbade illicit sexual relationships, and if one abstained from such sinful conduct, he was innocent. Jesus says that there is a higher standard which lays its demands upon men and women. It is the standard of God's Kingdom. It is a standard which cannot be formulated in terms of a legal code for it goes beyond the act to the intent. Before law, adultery is sin. Jesus says, "If in your heart there is lust, you stand before God as a guilty sinner in need of His forgiveness."

Do we dare to be honest with God's Word? There are probably few who will read these words who could be condemned as adulterers or adulteresses in the strict sense of the word. But God's Kingdom does not stop with externals; it pierces to our thoughts and imaginations, to the purposes of the mind and the heart. It goes to the very reservoirs of our being. Jesus says, If there is lust, if you look upon a woman with evil desire, you stand before God as a sinner. Righteousness, sexual purity, begins in the heart.

How modern this verse is! In a day when sin is glamorized, put on display, when our social habits thrust temptation upon us, we need to come back to the standards of old-fashioned Biblical righteousness and purity.

The imperative need for a pure heart is emphasized in the words that follow. "If your right eye causes you to sin, pluck it out and throw it away; it is better that you lose one of your members than that your whole body be thrown into hell" (v. 29). It is very important to note that this verse and those which immediately follow cannot possibly be interpreted with rigid literalness. You cannot satisfy the righteousness of the Sermon on the Mount alone by fulfilling the external letter of its teaching. Suppose your eye is constantly leading you into sin, and you read this verse and say, "I am determined to solve this problem. The Bible says that if my eye causes me to stumble, I should pluck it out." And in a burst of determination you jab a sharp stick into your eye and destroy it. Is your problem solved? Will you then be free from the sin of lust? You will experience great pain and suffering, but your real problem has not been touched, for sin lodges in the heart, not in the eye.

The same thing is true of the next verse. "And if your right hand causes you to sin, cut it off and throw it away; it is better that you lose one of your members than that your whole body should go into hell" (v. 30). Suppose you are constantly being led into sin by your hand, and you read this verse and forthwith say, "Here is the solution for my sin. I'll cut my hand off; then I will sin no more." Will that solve the problem? The problem is not in your hand but in the heart, in the mind.

What then does our Lord mean? If His words are not to be taken literally, how are we to understand them? They mean this:

that if lust is your besetting sin, do anything necessary to find the solution to the problem, whatever the cost may be. If plucking your eye out would solve the problem, do it. If cutting your hand off would solve the problem, do it. Do whatever you must. Do not play with sin, do not toy with temptation, or it will destroy you.

It is obvious that here again is a standard of righteousness which transcends the level of human attainment. Who is free from temper? Who is pure and free from lust? Taken out of context, these words only condemn us to perdition. No man in any dispensation can fulfil them. Yet it is the righteousness which God's Kingdom demands; and the righteousness which God demands of us, He must give to us, or we are lost. The only life which can be made pure is the life which knows the power of God's Kingdom, His rule. Furthermore, only those in whom God now exercises His rule will enter His future Kingdom. This saying, apart from the grace of God, is not salvation but condemnation.

We must notice verses 31 and 32. "It was also said, 'Whoever divorces his wife, let him give her a certificate of divorce.' But I say to you that every one who divorces his wife except on the ground of unchastity, makes her an adulteress; and whoever marries a divorced woman commits adultery." Here is a teaching which flies in the face of our modern conventions. Today divorce and remarriage are casual matters. The standards of marital morality are often determined by convenience, not by the Word of God. This unbiblical standard is pervading our entire culture. How often a man or a woman puts away his mate because he has grown tired of her or he has found a new infatuation. Such conduct is becoming almost a modern fashion. God's Word says that is sin. Jesus said there is one ground for divorce. When one party is unfaithful and breaks the marriage vow, in the sight of God the marriage bond is broken. The Old Testament condemned adultery with the death penalty (Lev. 20: 10). The New Testament says that an adulterer is to be considered as one dead, and the innocent party is freed from his marriage vows as though his mate had died. But divorce for the sake of marrying another is sin, for it is rooted in lust. Our generation needs to return to a Biblical standard of purity in the relationship between the sexes for the foundation of a stable family life. This is the righteousness that belongs to the Kingdom of God.

We next meet the Law of Honesty. "Again you have heard that it was said to men of old, 'You shall not swear falsely, but shall perform to the Lord what you have sworn.' But I say to you, Do not swear at all, either by heaven, for it is the throne of God, or by the earth, for it is his footstool, or by Jerusalem, for it is the city of the great King. And do not swear by your head, for you cannot make one hair white or black. Let what you say be simply 'Yes' or 'No'; any thing more than this comes from evil" (Matt. 5: 33–37).

It is possible to take these verses superficially in a literal interpretation of the letter and miss the meaning altogether. Some people feel they satisfy the teaching of the passage when they never let themselves be put under oath in a court of law. However, the formal oath taken in modern legal procedure is not the context of this teaching. The setting of our Lord's words is something quite different. The Jew of antiquity was quite ready to put himself under oath as a show of his alleged goodwill and fidelity. To the Jewish mind, various objects possessed differing degrees of holiness, and an oath was binding only to the degree that the object used in the oath was thought to be holy. Thus according to the scribal tradition, a man might bind himself by a succession of oaths and yet violate his word without guilt. Jewish casuistry reached its climax in the scribal discussion of the validity of various oaths. This made a mockery of the basic ethic of honesty. It is this historical situation which provides the background for our Lord's teaching. Jesus said, "Do not swear by heaven, nor by the earth, nor by Jerusalem, nor by thy head." These and many other objects were used in the taking of oaths.

What our Lord means is this: If you must take an oath before your word can be trusted, that very fact convicts you of being a sinner. The man who knows the righteousness of the Kingdom of God does not need an oath at all. His naked word is valid.

How modern this ancient teaching is. Its relevance is not found in the question of a formal oath in our legal processes. Here is a man who is punctilious about keeping the letter of his agreements, but if he can find a way to get around the letter and take an unfair advantage of his competitor, he prides himself for his cleverness.

Let the other fellow be smart enough to guard himself against that loophole! The righteousness of the Kingdom of God cuts squarely across such superficial hypocrisy. Let your word be your oath. When you say you will do something, let your neighbour be able to trust your word, both in the spirit and the letter of your promise. This is the Law of Honesty.

How the righteousness of the Kingdom, the Law of Honesty, tests our business ethics! In our competitive society, Christians often employ the world's standards in the conduct of their business rather than the standards of God's Kingdom! One would never know from the way some Christians conduct themselves in their business relationships that they knew anything about the righteousness of God. God wants us to bear our testimony with our lips; but even more important is what we are and how we live. "Except your righteousness exceeds that of the Scribes and Pharisees, ye shall never enter the kingdom of heaven."

Let us consider one more illustration of Kingdom righteousness: The Law of Love. "You have heard that it was said, 'An eye for an eye and a tooth for a tooth.' But I say to you, Do not resist one who is evil. But if any one smites you on the right cheek, turn to him the other also; and if any one would sue you and take your coat, let him have your cloak as well; and if any one forces you to go one mile, go with him two miles. Give to him who begs from you, and do not refuse him who would borrow from you" (vv. 38–43).

This teaching has been a stumbling-block to many. How can we possibly apply the Sermon on the Mount in this evil world and live by its standards? If any one interprets these words literally, he certainly cannot conduct a business venture or protect his own interests. Recently I passed through a small New England village where I lived as a boy, and I stopped at one of the two general stores to see a man whom I remembered from my boyhood. His name was on the sign over the door, but the store was locked up and inside all was confusion. I stopped at the other store up the street and asked, "What has happened to John X, that his store is locked up?" I was told that John had been too kind and generous. He trusted everybody. He gave such unlimited credit that he became bankrupt. He had to go out of business because of his debts.

Is this not what the Sermon on the Mount tells us to do? If we should obey it with wooden literalness, this would be the inevitable frequent result. If the Western nations literally practised non-resistance and liquidated all military resources, we would at once find ourselves under a world-wide tyranny of Communism. However, we have already discovered that our Lord sometimes uses radical metaphors which were not intended to be taken with rigid literalness. He was concerned with the condition of the heart, with the inner attitude of mind.

Along with what is said in this passage are some other principles which have never been abrogated. Paul under inspiration insists upon the principle of law and order. In Romans 13: 4-5, he asserts that judicial procedures are of divine origin. Furthermore, our Lord himself did not fulfil the letter of this verse if it be construed with wooden literalness. In John 18: 19 ff., the High Priest asked Jesus about his teaching, and Jesus said, "I have spoken openly to the world; I have always taught in synagogues and in the temple, where all Jews come together; I have said nothing secretly. Why do you ask me?" One of the officers standing by struck Jesus with his hand, and said, "Is that how you answer the high priest?" Jesus did not turn the other cheek; he rebuked His assailant with the words, "If I have spoken wrongly, bear witness to the wrong; but if I have spoken rightly, why do you strike me?" (v. 23).

We must therefore look beneath the letter of this teaching to discover its meaning. Furthermore, reflection will show that it would be possible to fulfil the letter of this teaching and yet completely miss our Lord's true meaning. You have heard about the pacifist who believed in physical non-resistance. He and a friend were walking down the street one day when the pacifist fell into a discussion with a third man which led to a quarrel. His opponent hit him in the face, and the pacifist literally turned the other cheek and was struck again. Thereupon he turned and walked away. His friend said to him, "I do not see how you could exercise such magnificent self-control to let yourself be struck twice. How do you do it?" The pacifist said, "I turned the other cheek, but you did not see how I was boiling inside." What he really wanted to do was to return blow for blow. He did not know the righteousness he professed.

Now, let us not be misunderstood. There are many situations where one will fulfil the very letter of this teaching. It is very possible that the context of this passage is to be found in an earlier saying of our Lord, "Blessed are those who are persecuted *for righteousness' sake*" (Matt. 5: 10). There come times when men will persecute you because you are a follower of the Lord Jesus (and notice that in Matt. 5: 10-11, the primary emphasis is upon persecution by word of mouth, not physical violence). You will meet opposition; and sometimes bodily harm will befall you because you are a disciple of Jesus Christ. This does not often happen in so-called Christian countries; but in other lands, Christians still suffer physical persecution. When a follower of Jesus meets persecution because he is a disciple, he will never fight back. A missionary friend wrote that he had recently had some expensive dental bridgework done. One day as he was distributing Christian literature, he found himself faced by an angry crowd which threatened bodily violence. His first thought was, "Ought I not to protect my new bridgework?" He was not concerned about fighting back, but he was concerned about his financial investment. But he concluded, "No, I'll leave it to the Lord," and he elected the course of non-resistance. Incidentally, he did not lose his bridgework.

There will indeed be times like this when one will fulfil the letter of the law of love. But that is not the only element or even the most important element in this passage; for the righteousness about which our Lord was speaking is a righteousness of the heart. The righteousness of the Kingdom of God demands an attitude of heart which is not motivated by selfish concerns, which does not demand even one's legitimate rights. Our Lord looks for a complete freedom from any spirit of personal revenge. When one does you a wrong, when one speaks ill of you, when one has offended you, what is your reaction? The reaction of the natural man, the reaction of the moral man, even of the religious man, is to get even and to square the account. This is not the righteousness of God's Kingdom. God's righteousness manifests itself in a heart attitude which is motivated by love for him who has done the wrong and which is free from the motivation of personal vindication.

The illustrations our Lord gives are radical instances of the expression of love. This love extends even to our enemies. "You have heard that it was said, 'You shall love your neighbour and hate your enemy.' But I say to you, Love your enemies" (vv. 43–44). Yes, love your enemies; not merely your friends or your kind neighbours, or even those who are neutral towards you; but love those who do you wrong. Love those who deliberately harm you. This is the supreme test of Christian character. I have seen situations where people in the Church of God do not put this principle into practice among themselves. I have witnessed among God's people bitterness and rancour and animosity and hostility and enmity. This is a denial of our true character. Jesus says, Your attitude, your actions must always be motivated by love. Complete freedom from the spirit of revenge and of self-vindication, returning love for hatred, repaying kindness for evil—this is the righteousness of God's Kingdom.

This love is not primarily a feeling or an emotion; it is concern in action. Love seeks the best welfare of the objects of its concern. The classic portrayal of Christian love is I Corinthians 13; and when Paul would describe what love *is*, he tells us how love *works*. "Love is patient and kind." Love is goodwill in action. Love is concern in expression. We know from other teachings of God's Word that love may sometimes chastise and discipline. "Whom the Lord loveth, he chasteneth" (Heb. 12:6, A.V.). Love does not mean the abandonment of justice and right; nor is it a sentimental benevolence which does not have the capacity for holy wrath. Our human problem rests in the difficulty—shall we say the impossibility—of extricating elements of personal pique and selfish vindication from holy wrath.

Our Lord's teaching has to do with the springs of one's personal reaction and character. Love seeks the best welfare even of its enemies. It can return a curse with a blessing. It can repay violence with gentleness. It can reward a wrong with kindness. It can act in this way because it is not motivated by a spirit of vengefulness but of concern for the other man. This is the righteousness of God's Kingdom.

A supreme manifestation of this law of love is found in forgiveness. Jesus taught us to pray, "Forgive us our debts, as we forgive our debtors" (Matt. 6: 12, A.V.). You can truly forgive a man only when you act in love. If you do not look upon him with love, you do not really forgive, even though you profess to do so.

Someone may say, "This petition is not a Christian prayer. It is talking about a transaction with God. We ask God to forgive us in the measure and the degree to which we have forgiven others. This reflects a legal righteousness, not the righteousness of grace through faith. Christians pray, Forgive us freely for Christ's sake."

Let us think this through. If the righteousness of the Kingdom of God is a righteousness of human works, we must at once admit that the prayer has no application to anyone. Human nature does not forgive like that. It does not matter in what dispensation you look, you cannot find unregenerate human nature which will produce conduct like that demanded in the Sermon on the Mount. If this verse is based on legalistic ground, then anyone who attempts to live by it is condemned. We need God's *perfect* forgiveness; and it is not human nature to forgive like that.

The Word of God has a way of explaining itself. In Matthew 18, our Lord explains what this forgiveness means. Peter had been troubled by Jesus' teaching about forgiveness. How could anyone forgive so completely? Finally, he came to the Lord and said to him, "Lord, how often shall my brother sin against me, and I forgive him? As many as seven times?" (v. 21). Now seven is not a very large number, is it? But let us consider this situation. If somebody offends us in the same way seven times in succession, can we honestly forgive him the same insult seven times? This is not a trivial offence.

But hear what our Lord says, "I do not say to you seven times, but seventy times seven" (v. 22). Seventy times seven? How many is that? Four hundred and ninety. Suppose someone called you a vile name four hundred and ninety times in succession. Every day, at 9.30 a.m., a business associate who dislikes you comes into your office, stands before your desk and curses you, four hundred and ninety times. That is nearly two years of working days. Could you forgive him? Would you want to forgive him? Only a heart filled with the grace of God could forgive like that.

Jesus illustrated the quality of forgiveness demanded by the

Kingdom of God by a parable. "Therefore the kingdom of heaven may be compared to a king who wished to settle accounts with his servants. When he began the reckoning, one was brought to him who owed him ten thousand talents." In modern terms, that would be about ten million dollars. Here was a man in a hopeless situation. His burden of debt was so great that he had no hope of ever settling his affairs and meeting the debt. He was bankrupt. "And as he could not pay, his lord ordered him to be sold, with his wife and children and all that he had, and payment to be made" (v. 25). This was the ancient method of dealing with debtors. Bankruptcy meant not only the liquidation of all business resources; it included the liquidation of all personal resources and property; and beyond that, a man's wife, his children, and the debtor himself were sold into slavery that every possible asset might be realized by the creditor against the debt.

"So the servant fell on his knees, imploring, 'Lord, have patience with me, and I will pay you everything'" (v. 26). The debtor begged for mercy and forgiveness, and even though he knew he could never pay the debt, he promised to do so. "And out of pity for him the lord of that servant released him and forgave him the debt" of ten million dollars. What amazing kindness!

"But that same servant, as he went out, came upon one of his fellow servants who owed him a hundred *denarii*." A hundred *denarii* is twenty dollars. While this was a substantial sum of money in that day, it was one which a man could repay in time. Ten million dollars of debt, twenty dollars of credit. He had just been forgiven this staggering ten million dollar debt; and he was then confronted by a fellow servant who owed him a mere twenty dollars. "And seizing him by the throat he said, 'Pay what you owe.' So his fellow servant fell down and besought him, 'Have patience with me, and I will pay you.' He refused and went and put him in prison till he should pay the debt" (vv. 28-30).

Word of the unforgiving spirit of the forgiven servant came to the ears of his master. "Then his lord summoned him and said to him, 'You wicked servant! I forgave you all that debt because you besought me; and should not you have had mercy on your fellow servant, as I had mercy on you?' And in anger his lord delivered him to the jailors, till he should pay all his debt" (vv.

32–34). Then our Lord adds these sobering words: "So also my heavenly Father will do to every one of you, if you do not forgive your brother from your heart" (v. 35).

Yes, we do pray, "Forgive us our debts, as we forgive those who sin against us." In this parable of forgiveness, notice one thing: God's forgiveness precedes and conditions my forgiveness of my fellow. The point of the parable rests in this fact. Human forgiveness is to be grounded upon and motivated by the divine forgiveness. My willingness to forgive is the measure of the reality of my profession that I have been forgiven. If I say that the Lord has forgiven me the twenty-million dollar debt of my sin, and yet I cannot forgive some brother a mere twenty dollars of a relatively trivial offence against myself, I make a mockery of my Christian profession. There is no reality in such a self-contradictory religion. Yes, we *must* pray, Forgive us as we forgive.

This is the law of love; this is the Gospel of the Kingdom. The righteousness of the Kingdom is a righteousness which only God Himself can give. Perfect purity, perfect honesty, perfect love, perfect forgiveness: what man is there anywhere in any dispensation who can live such a life? If the righteousness of the Kingdom is a standard which I must attain in my own ability, I stand *for ever* condemned and shut out of the Kingdom of God. No one, Jew or Gentile, by human merit can attain the standard of the Sermon on the Mount. The righteousness which God's Kingdom demands, God's Kingdom must give. It must be of grace or I am lost. Our Lord's own illustration of forgiveness shows that this is the divine order. I can really forgive only as I know God's forgiveness. I can manifest the life of the Kingdom only as I have experienced it. But as we have discovered in our earlier studies, God's Kingdom has entered into the present evil Age and we may experience its life, its righteousness.

The righteousness of the Sermon on the Mount is the righteousness of the man who has experienced the reign of God in his life. This is the standard by which the disciple of the Lord Jesus is to live. He will attain it in so far as he has experienced the sovereign reign of God. He is to seek an experience which is completely under divine direction. The beginning of this experience is found in the new birth. Jesus said to Nicodemus, "Unless one is born anew, he cannot see the kingdom of God" (John 3: 3). When one submits himself to the reign of God, the miracle of the new birth takes place within his heart. The Holy Spirit creates new life. As a new creature, the servant of God's rule will experience a real and evident measure of the righteousness of God's Kingdom in this evil Age. This is not stated but is assumed in the Sermon on the Mount. The righteousness of the Kingdom is a manifestation of the life of the Kingdom. Just as the fulness of life, which belongs to The Age to Come, has become a present blessing, so the righteousness of the Kingdom belongs to The Age to Come, but has been imparted to the sons of the Kingdom through Christ and the Holy Spirit.

CHAPTER VII

THE DEMAND OF THE KINGDOM

T HE Kingdom of God offers to men divine blessings—the blessings of The Age to Come. The study thus far has been devoted to an exposition of these blessings. Our Lord began His ministry with the announcement, "The kingdom of God is at hand. Repent, and believe in the good news." We have found that the Kingdom of God is God's redemptive reign. It is God's conquest through the person of Christ over His enemies: sin, Satan, and death. God's Kingdom is manifested in several great acts. At the Second Coming of Christ, His Kingdom will appear in power and glory. But this glorious Kingdom of God, which will be manifested at Christ's return has already entered into history, but without the outward glory. The future has invaded the present. The Kingdom of God which is yet to come in power and in glory has already come in a secret and hidden form to work among men and within them. The power of God's Kingdom which in The Age to Come will sweep away both evil and all its influence has come among men in the present evil Age to deliver them from the power of sin, from servitude to Satan, and from the bondage and fear of death. The life of God's Kingdom which will be realized in its fulness when Christ comes, when our very bodies shall be redeemed—that life of the future Kingdom has entered into the present so that men may now be born again and enter into God's Kingdom—the sphere of His reign, the realm of His blessings. The Holy Spirit who one day will completely transform us so that we become like the Lord Jesus Christ in His glorified body has come to us before the arrival of the New Age to dwell within our hearts, to give us the life of the Kingdom here and now that we may enjoy fellowship with God. Tomorrow is here today. The future has already begun. We have tasted the life, the powers, the blessings of The Age to Come.

The question remains: How does one enter into that experience?

What demand does God's Kingdom lay upon us? How does one receive this life? How is the righteousness of the Kingdom to be obtained? How does one find the indwelling of God's Spirit imparting the life of the future Age?

The Word of God comes to us with a very simple answer. Indeed, its very simplicity involves a profound difficulty. While it is simple, it nevertheless reaches down into the very depths of our being. To the Romans, Paul wrote, "If you confess with your lips that Jesus is Lord and believe in your heart that God raised him from the dead, you will be saved" (Rom. 10: 9). To the jailor at Philippi, Paul said, "Believe in the Lord Jesus, and you will be saved" (Acts 16: 31). The Fourth Gospel constantly reiterates the purpose of the book: "These are written that you may believe that Jesus is the Christ, the Son of God, and that believing you may have life in his name" (John 20: 31).

Is the Kingdom of heaven to be entered merely by taking the name of Jesus upon one's lips and making a verbal confession? Is the blessing of life to be received by believing in the resurrection and deity of Christ? Can a creed save me? Can the utterance of three words, "Jesus is Lord," bestow life upon me? What does it mean to confess Jesus as Lord?—to believe in the Lord Jesus? The answer may be found in the demand of the Kingdom of God. The Kingdom makes one fundamental demand: the demand for decision. In Christ, the Kingdom now confronts us. The life of The Age to Come now stands before us. The One who shall tomorrow be the Judge of all men has already come into history. He faces us with one demand: decision. Bultmann is right when he says that Jesus proclaimed the nearness of God as The Demander. Jesus' message was, "Repent, for the kingdom of heaven is at hand." The basic meaning of "repentance" is to turn around, to reverse the course of life, to change the whole direction of action, to turn and to embrace in decision the Kingdom of God.

Life is made up of decisions. The course of every man's life is determined by his decisions. One might say that the difference between the success of two men who are equally talented is determined by the way in which they make decisions. The adequacy of one's decisions, the intelligence with which they are made, and the ability, once a good decision has been made, to rest upon it and to move forward to the next important step will often decide the measure of success or failure. Some people go through life vacillating, wavering, unsure of themselves, never able to say a distinct Yes or No. These are people who never accomplish anything worth while for themselves or their fellow men, but who dissipate life and energy in inner conflict and indecision.

The essence of repentance is a decision which determines the quality of present life and future destiny.

As Jesus was about to leave Galilee for the last time, he sent seventy disciples to preach the Gospel of the Kingdom throughout all the countryside. The injunction He laid upon His ambassadors was this: "Heal the sick in it and say to them, 'The kingdom of God has come near to you'" (Luke 10: 9). The Kingdom of God came into these villages in the person of the emissaries of our Lord. These preachers looked like ordinary people, Galilean fishermen; yet they were bearers of the Kingdom of God. How would the residents of these cities react? They could either welcome the emissaries of Christ and thereby receive the Kingdom itself; or if they chose, they could reject it. But this rejection would be a terrible thing. "But whenever you enter a town and they do not receive you, go into its streets and say, 'Even the dust of your town that clings to our feet, we wipe off against you; nevertheless know this, that the kingdom of God has come near.' I tell you, it shall be more tolerable on that day for Sodom than for that town"—because it had refused the Kingdom of God (vv. 10–12).

The basic demand of the Kingdom is a response of man's will. Men must receive it. They must yield to it. God's Kingdom does not ask us to find in ourselves the righteousness that it demands; God will give us the righteousness of his Kingdom. God's Kingdom does not ask us to create the life that it requires; God's Kingdom will give us that life. God's Kingdom does not set up a standard and say, "When you achieve this standard of righteousness, you may enter the Kingdom." God's Kingdom makes one demand: Repent! Turn! Decide! Receive the Kingdom; for as you receive it, you receive its life, you receive its blessing, you receive the destiny reserved for those who embrace it.

As we study this demand for decision in our Lord's teaching,

G

we find that it cannot be taken lightly. Jesus required of men a *resolute* decision. This is set forth in Luke 9: 57. "As they were going along the road, a man said to him, 'I will follow you wherever you go.'" Here was a man who seemed ready to make the decision to follow Christ. In response, Jesus said, "Foxes have holes, and birds of the air have nests; but the Son of man has nowhere to lay his head" (v. 58). Jesus challenged the seriousness of this decision. Do you know what your decision involves? Are you willing to become a disciple of one who is homeless, who has no standing and no prestige? Have you thought it through? Have you considered its implications? Jesus demanded a resolute decision, an intelligent decision, one not lightly made.

Again, Jesus said to another, "Follow me." But he said, "Lord, let me first go and bury my father" (Luke 9: 59). Here was a man who professed readiness to make a decision, but there was something else to be done first. "Yes, I want to follow, but wait a bit. There is a prior claim upon me. Let me first care for it, and then I will follow. I have good intentions, but just give me time." But Jesus replied in words which seem harsh unless taken in their context, "Leave those who are spiritually dead to bury those who are physically dead." I am interpreting the verse now. "Leave the dead to bury their own dead; but as for you, go and proclaim the kingdom of God" (v. 60). The Kingdom of God demands immediate, urgent decision. When the claim comes to you, you cannot trifle with it. You may think, First, I must live my life. First, there is a career to be pursued. I have important plans for my future which must first be carried out. I have obligations which I must first discharge. No! Jesus said there must be an immediate decision which is resolute and unqualified.

Again, another said, "Lord, I will follow thee." Yes, I recognize I ought to embrace the Kingdom of God, that I should become a disciple; "but let me first say farewell to those at my home" (Luke 9: 61). On the surface, this was a reasonable request. If a man is to leave home to devote his life to discipleship to Jesus, it is fitting and proper that he take farewell of his family. But we must interpret this saying in its context. Jesus said unto him, "No one who puts his hand to the plough and looks back is fit for the kingdom of God" (v. 62). Here was a man who professed willingness to make a decision, but he was reluctant. Jesus says, There is no room for reluctance. If you respond to the Kingdom of God and its claims upon your life, there must be no hesitation, no looking back. One cannot try to hold on to what he has left behind him. One cannot cling to the past. There must be no uncertainty as to whether one is prepared to go all the way. "No one who puts his hand to the plough and looks back is fit for the kingdom of God." The Kingdom of God demands a resolute decision, an irrevocable decision, a clean-cut decision.

Furthermore, the Kingdom demands *radical* decision. Some decisions are easily made and require little effort; but the decision for the Kingdom of God is often difficult and requires great energy of the will. Jesus said, "From the days of John the Baptist until now the kingdom of heaven works mightily, and men of violence take it by force" (Matt. 11: 12). This saying has received many diverse interpretations, but we may follow Luke's understanding of it. "The law and the prophets were until John; since then the good news of the kingdom of God is preached, and every one enters it violently" (Luke 16: 16). The Kingdom demands a response so radical that it may be described in terms of violence and force.

How are we to understand these words? What does violence have to do with receiving God's Kingdom? Our Lord Himself illustrated this demand more than once. "And if your eye causes you to sin, pluck it out; it is better for you to enter the kingdom of God with one eye than with two eyes to be thrown into hell" (Mark 9: 47; see also vv. 43–46). Here is indeed violence: the plucking out of an eye, the cutting off of a hand or foot, in order to enter the Kingdom of God.

"Do not think that I have come to bring peace on earth; I have not come to bring peace, but a sword" (Matt. 10: 34). A sword is an instrument of violence. Sometimes decision for the Kingdom will be a sword which cuts across other relations bringing pain and suffering. Indeed, "if any one comes to me and does not hate his own father and mother and wife . . . he cannot be my disciple" (Luke 14: 26). Hatred: this is a word of violence.

"Strive to enter by the narrow door" (Luke 13: 24). The Greek word is a strong term from which the English word "agonize" is derived and means "to strain every nerve." It is the common word used to describe the physical conflict in athletic games. Here again is violence, striving, intense effort.

All of this metaphorical language describes the radical character of the decision demanded by the Kingdom of God. The modern man is usually quite casual about his religion. He will often undertake radical measures in the pursuit of wealth, success, power; but he is unwilling to become deeply moved about the concerns of his soul. Jesus says that such a man cannot know the life of the Kingdom. It demands a response, a radical decision, an enthusiastic reception. Nominalism is the curse of modern western Christianity. Jesus' disciples must be radicals in their unqualified enthusiasm for the life of God's Kingdom.

The decision which God's Kingdom demands is also a *costly* decision. A rich young ruler came to Jesus with the question, "Teacher, what good deed must I do, to have eternal life?" (Matt. 19: 16). There are few men who in their more sober moments have not asked themselves this question. There is a hunger for life within the human heart. This life, as verse 23 proves, is the life of the Kingdom of God. It is the question of salvation (v. 25). This young man was expressing the deep desire which all men possess—the desire to find life, eternal life, in a realm beyond this earthly existence which is hemmed in by sin and death.

After ascertaining his sincerity, Jesus faced him with the fundamental issue: decision. "Come, follow me" (v. 21). There is the issue. Turn about! Leave your old life. Receive the Kingdom. Follow me!

In this case, this decision was not a simple or easy matter, for it involved great cost. Jesus said something to this young man he is never recorded to have said to another. He looked into his heart and saw what was holding him back from making this decision. The young man was rich; and Jesus perceived that he was attached to his wealth. Therefore Jesus said, "Your decision for the Kingdom of God must be unqualified. Your wealth is standing in your way. Therefore, go and sell everything you have, and you will then be free to follow me."

It should be clear that liquidation of wealth of itself would not make this young man a disciple. Discipleship, decision was lodged in the demand, "Follow me." The man could have become a pauper and still have remained outside the Kingdom had he not followed Jesus. Disposition of wealth was not itself discipleship; but in this case it was a necessary prelude to discipleship. Jesus demanded the removal of a barrier. Anything, whether wealth or career or family, which stands in the way or decision must yield before the claims of God's Kingdom.

Jesus laid no universal demand for poverty upon men. His concern against the laying up of wealth upon earth in the Sermon on the Mount (Matt. 6: 19) is not to bring men into poverty but to deliver them from a false security. Men think that by the accumulation of wealth they will free themselves from anxiety. Jesus said that they only add other anxieties which are involved in the fear of the loss of their wealth. Poverty itself is no virtue. Jesus' demand is for decision, for submission to God and His Kingdom. Wealth is evil when it stands in the way of such decision. So Jesus said, "Young man, you have a barrier. You love your wealth and all the comforts and good things it brings to you. It commands your affection. That affection must give way to a higher loyalty—to the Kingdom of God."

This remains true. The demand of the Kingdom is still a costly decision. If wealth, position, influence, or ambition command a man's loyalty so that his life is directed to the attainment of personal ends, whether material or social, rather than the glory of God, his life must have a new centre of orientation. Every other interest must become secondary and subservient to the rule of God. The issue relates itself fundamentally to a man's will and to the objectives he chooses to serve.

I have seen young men who appeared to be Christians of great promise who became possessed by driving personal ambition. A struggle ensued between the claims of God and ambition, and a choice was made. When the choice was for self-advancement rather than for God's Kingdom, love for the things of God withered.

The proper attitude of a disciple of Jesus to material blessings is beautifully illustrated by the Apostle Paul. Paul had been "delivered . . . from the domination of darkness and transferred . . . to the kingdom of his beloved Son" (Col. 1: 13). Paul was living for the Kingdom of God, which was not "food and drink but righteousness and peace and joy in the Holy Spirit" (Rom.

14: 17). Because Paul had experienced the life of the Kingdom of God, he had acquired a new conception of the place and importance of possessions. "I have learned, in whatever state I am, to be content. I know how to be abased, and I know how to abound; in any and all circumstances I have learned the secret of facing plenty and hunger, abundance and want. I can do all things in him who strengthens me" (Phil. 4: 11-13). Paul had been initiated into a secret of contentment, because his happiness and his security did not depend upon externals. If he was in want, he did not feel God had forsaken him. If he experienced abundance, he did not become so attached to his abundance that his happiness depended upon it. His security was in "him who strengthens me" —in the Lord.

This experience is essential for every one who would know the blessings of God's Kingdom. For the rich young man, life did not consist of "righteousness and peace and joy"; he knew nothing of the Kingdom of God. Life consisted of "food and drink," of the things his wealth could buy. His first love was his wealth and all it represented. Nevertheless, he was not satisfied. He did not know contentment. This unsatisfied hunger brought him to Jesus with his question about eternal life. However, when faced with the alternatives, he made the wrong choice. He was unwilling to cut loose from his dependence upon his wealth and material resources.

God may not always require a man to forsake his wealth, but He does demand that he forsake *love* of possessions. God demands a decision of the will which entails a willingness actually to forsake wealth if He should so lead. The question is one of affection. A child of the Kingdom will receive the good things of the physical realm as gifts from a loving father (Matt. 6: 26-30) and will be thankful. But his love, his dependence, his security rest in the Giver and in God's Kingdom, not in the gifts. He will seek first God's Kingdom and trust God to provide what is needed for his daily life (Matt. 6: 33-34). The rich young man did not dare trust God. He trusted only his wealth. Therefore it was necessary for him to free himself of this false security before he could give himself to God and His Kingdom. He had to decide; for the Kingdom demands decision, costly decision.

Sometimes this decision may cost the affection of loved ones.

This is apparent from the instructions Jesus gave his disciples as he prepared them for their ministry. They were to announce that the Kingdom of God had come near in their own proclamation (Matt. 10: 7). A demand was laid upon their audience: to receive the emissaries of the Kingdom and thereby to receive the message of the Kingdom, indeed, the King Himself. "He who receives you receives me, and he who receives me receives him who sent me" (Matt. 10: 40). In some instances, this would be a costly decision; for it would cause the rupture of normal family ties. "Do not think that I have come to bring peace on earth: I have not come to bring peace, but a sword. For I have come to set a man against his father, and a daughter against her mother, and a daughter-in-law against her mother-in-law; and a man's foes will be those of his own household. He who loves father or mother more than me is not worthy of me; and he who loves son or daughter more than me is not worthy of me" (Matt. 10: 34–37).

Does this mean that when one becomes a Christian, human affection has no further place in his life? When one follows Christ, must he sever all his family ties? Surely this is not required. In fact, the opposite is often true. When a man and a woman have shared a human affection which is in turn sanctified by a mutual love for God and His Kingdom, they are the happiest people on earth.

There is, however, a stern truth here. When a human relationship stands in the way of the demand of God's Kingdom, there can be but one choice. If the demand of the Kingdom has confronted you, but your father or your mother, or even if your husband or your wife says, "No, I'll not have it; you cannot follow Christ and have my affection," then there is only one decision which can be made: for God and His Kingdom. Even if human affection and family ties are shattered, the claims of God's Kingdom have priority.

We are thankful to God that in our culture with its Christian heritage, we are infrequently called upon to pay such a price. Fortunate is the child who has Christian parents praying for his salvation from birth, indeed from before birth. Blessed is the man, blessed is the woman, who has a wife or husband who shares a deep faith in the Lord, who can pray together and who share a common love for the things of God. Unfortunately, it is not always so. Sometimes, there comes a crisis. A decision must be made: for God or for family. In such times of decision, Jesus says that it must be a costly decision.

Again, the Kingdom of God may cost a man his very life. In Matthew 10: 38 Jesus said, "He who does not take his cross and follow me is not worthy of me." Here is the ultimate cost of decision.

What does it mean to take one's cross? People often talk about the difficult of cross-bearing. What a cross I have to carry! I have a physical burden, I suffer from migraine headaches or ulcers; I have arthritis, or rheumatism. What a cross of physical weakness and pain is laid upon me!

Others talk of the cross they must bear because of problems they have to face. My husband is short-tempered: what a cross I have to carry in putting up with his disposition! Others say, My cross is the necessity of working in an environment that is not Christian. I hear profanity and uncleanness day after day. What a heavy cross I must carry!

Such experiences are not crosses. They are burdens; and some-times burdens may be crushing. But a cross is not a burden; a cross is a place of death. Don't talk about bearing the burden of a cross. When you take up your cross, you are ready to die.

On another occasion, Jesus said, "Let him deny himself" (Luke 9: 23). Deny himself what? Candy before Easter? Tobacco during Lent? Something you want to do but don't think you ought to? Or does it mean self-denial, personal sacrifice to promote the Gospel?

Denial of self does not mean that I am to deny myself *things*. It means to deny *myself*, not to deny things to myself. "If any man would come after me, let him deny himself and take up his cross . . ." (Luke 9: 23). Self-denial is self-centred; denial of self is Christ-centred. Denial of self means death, nothing less. A cross is an instrument of death. Obviously, the saying does not mean that every Christian must suffer physical death. It does mean, however (and we speak carefully), that every disciple of Jesus must be ready to die. If we find ourselves in a situation where a choice has to be made between death and loyalty to Christ and His Kingdom, we shall be prepared to choose death. There are people in this evil Age who are paying the price of their lives and are spilling their blood because they love Jesus Christ and have responded to the demand of His Kingdom.

This is what cross-bearing means: a readiness to die with and for Christ. It means complete dedication to Christ, even though this dedication costs one his life. It means an act of self-surrender which holds nothing back, not even life itself. It means that my life, my will, my ambitions, my desires, my hopes—all are given to Christ. It means that I count myself as dead that Christ may live and reign in me. Paul expresses the same fundamental thought when he says, "I have been crucified with Christ; and it is no longer I who live, but Christ who lives in me" (Gal. 2: 20).

The taking up of the cross is something which takes place in the depths of the human spirit and is fundamental to one's relationship to Christ. If I am ready to die for Christ, then my life is not my own, it is His. My life belongs to Him together with all that life includes. Cross-bearing involves the question of lordship, rulership, of kingship. Christ cannot rule my life until I count myself dead, crucified. There can be only one ruler in my life: self or Christ. When I take up my cross and die, Christ can rule.

This principle of cross-bearing is illustrated by one of our seminary students who was preparing for a ministry of evangelistic music. He had received a musical training in one of America's outstanding schools of music and was an accomplished pianist. He loved his music, and when God called him into the ministry of the Gospel, he was happy at the prospect of using his musical gifts and training to serve the Lord. However, during the course of his seminary preparation God spoke to his heart. Suppose God wanted him in the ministry of preaching or teaching the Word rather than the ministry of music? Was he not dictating to God the terms of his ministry? Did he love his music more than he loved the Lord? Had he really surrendered his love for music to the Lord? Had he surrendered *himself*? A severe struggle ensued in his soul. Who was his master, Christ or music? He found release from the struggle only when he gave his music to the Lord and promised to serve in whatever way the Lord should lead, with or without music. In other words, he had to crucify his love for music. Indeed, he had to crucify *himself*, his will, his desires, before he had victory in his life. After he had given his love of music to the Lord, God gave it back to him, and he is today serving God as a missionary, using his musical gifts to glorify God. But first, he had to make a radical decision—a decision that involved his greatest human affection.

Finally, the Kingdom demands an *eternal* decision. The decision for or against the Kingdom of God in the present determines a man's future destiny. Jesus said, "Everyone who confesses me before men, the Son of man also will confess before the angels of God; but he who denies me before men will be denied before the angels of God" (Luke 12: 8–9). "For whoever is ashamed of me and of my words in this adulterous and sinful generation, of him will the Son of man also be ashamed, when he comes in the glory of his Father with the holy angels" (Mark 8: 38). There is to be a day of judgment, a day of separation among men. Christ one day will appear as the Son of man in glory to bring salvation to the sons of the Kingdom and a just condemnation to the sons of darkness. The Kingdom of God will then appear in power and glory.

But in His grace, God has sent His Son among men in advance of that day. Christ has come among us to confront us with the blessings and the demands of God's Kingdom. "Repent, for the kingdom of heaven has come near." Receive it! We may make a decision for that future Kingdom long before it comes in glory and judgment, because He who will be the future Judge has appeared among men to offer to them the life and blessing of that Kingdom here and now. The Kingdom demands decision as it confronts men—eternal decision. Tomorrow has met today. The Age to Come has entered This Age. The life of tomorrow is offered to us in the here and now. Heaven, if you please, has kissed the earth. What are we to do? One thing. The Kingdom of heaven has come near. Repent! Turn around, and receive the Good News. Surrender to its rule. This is the demand of the Kingdom.

CHAPTER VIII

THE KINGDOM, ISRAEL, AND THE CHURCH

THE most difficult aspect of the Biblical teaching of the Kingdom of God is its relationship to Israel and the Church. The difficulty rests in the fact that this relationship is not explicitly set forth in Scripture but must be inferred. As a result, utterly divergent interpretations have been suggested by equally devout students of the Bible.

The preceding chapters have expounded the thesis that the Kingdom of God in the New Testament is the redemptive work of God active in history for the defeat of His enemies, bringing to men the blessings of the divine reign. This approach enables us to interpret consistently the question of Israel and the Church in the New Testament.

It cannot be denied that Jesus offered the Kingdom to Israel. When he sent his disciples upon their preaching mission, he told them not to go among the Gentiles but to "go rather to the lost sheep of the house of Israel" (Matt. 10: 6). Jesus rebuffed a Canaanitish woman with the words, "I was sent only to the lost sheep of the house of Israel" (Matt. 15: 24). Furthermore, our Lord spoke of the Jews as the "sons of the Kingdom" (Matt. 8: 12), even though they were rejecting the Messiah and the Kingdom of God. They were the sons of the Kingdom because it was Israel whom God had chosen and to whom He had promised the blessings of the Kingdom. The Kingdom was theirs by right of election, history, and heritage. So it was that our Lord directed His ministry to them and offered to them that which had been promised them. When Israel rejected the Kingdom, the blessings which should have been theirs were given to those who would accept them.

This is seen in the sequence of verses in Matthew 11. The age of the law and the prophets ended with John the Baptist; since then the Kingdom of heaven has been at work among men. This is the most likely meaning of Matt. 11: 12–13. Verse 13 clearly states that the "prophets and the law prophesied until John"; and verse 12 says, "From the days of John the Baptist until now the kingdom of heaven has been coming violently, and men of violence take it by force." Such is the rendering in the margin of the Revised Standard Version, and it is the preferable rendition. The Kingdom of God, as we have seen, is God's reign redemptively at work among men; and this is the meaning of Matt. 11: 12. However, that generation of Israel would not respond to the work of God's Kingdom, either when John the Baptist preached repentance in anticipation of the Kingdom or when our Lord offered the blessings of the Kingdom. They were like obstinate children who were playing a game of imitation; they refused to play either wedding or funeral (vv. 16–17). They refused the sombre challenge of John to repent, and they declined the joyful offer of Jesus of the power and the life of God's Kingdom.

Therefore, only judgment is in store for that generation (v. 20). A terrible woe is pronounced over the cities of Israel like Chorazin and Bethsaida because mighty works had been performed in their streets—the mighty works of the Kingdom of God itself. Jesus had appeared in their cities, casting out demons, delivering men from satanic power and preaching that the Kingdom of God had come upon them to defeat Satan and to deliver men from his rule. Yet in spite of these mighty works, Israel did not respond. Therefore, "it shall be more tolerable on the day of judgment for the land of Sodom than for you" (v. 24).

The invitation to receive the blessings of the Kingdom is offered to those who will accept it on an individual basis. Jesus said, "Come to me, all who labour and are heavy-laden, and I will give you rest. Take my yoke upon you, and learn from me; for I am gentle and lowly in heart, and you will find rest for your souls" (vv. 28–29).

In the Old Testament dispensation, God had dealt with Israel primarily as a family and a nation and had given to His people both earthly and religious blessings. When God made a covenant with Abraham, Abraham took all the male members of his household and circumcised them, thus bringing them within the terms and blessings of the covenant (Gen. 17: 22–27). Although

THE KINGDOM, ISRAEL AND THE CHURCH 109

we find in the prophets a growing emphasis upon the individual, the terms of the Old Covenant were primarily with Israel as a nation; and Gentiles could share the spiritual blessings of the Covenant only by becoming part of the nation.

Our Lord's offer of the Kingdom of God was not the offer of a political kingdom, nor did it involve national and material blessings. The Jews wanted a political king to overthrow their enemies; but Jesus refused an earthly crown (John 6: 15), offering spiritual bread instead of an earthly kingdom (John 6: 52-57). Jesus addressed Himself to the individual; and the terms of the new relationship were exclusively those of personal decision and faith. This fact is eloquently set forth in the preparatory ministry of John the Baptist who told the Jews that descent from Abraham was not adequate to qualify them for the blessings of the coming Kingdom (Matt. 3: 7-10). The spiritual blessings of the new era were to be bestowed on an individual rather than on a family basis. Even those who considered themselves children of the Old Covenant must experience personal repentance and submit to baptism in anticipation of Him who was to come.

Our Lord also made the personal terms of the new relationship clear when he said, "Do not think that I have come to bring peace on earth; I have not come to bring peace, but a sword. For I have come to set a man against his father, and a daughter against her mother, and a daughter-in-law against her mother-in-law: and a man's foes will be those of his own household" (Matt. 10: 35-36). The family unit is no longer to be the basis of the relationship between God and man; personal faith which would often cut across family lines and even rupture ties of flesh and blood is the fundamental basis of man's relationship to the Kingdom of God.

The Jews as a whole refused this new relationship. There were some, however, who responded and who became disciples of our Lord and thus true sons of the Kingdom of God. These formed the nucleus of what became the Church.

The sixteenth chapter of Matthew relates our Lord's purpose in the formation of the new people of God, the Church. It is significant that Jesus could say nothing about His redemptive purpose to bring into existence this new people of God until the disciples had realized that He was indeed the Messiah. Confession of His Messiahship is at the same time confession of the presence of the Kingdom of God, for it is the mission of the Messiah to bring the Kingdom of God to men. At this point, we must understand that there was for the disciples a problem in the recognition of our Lord's Messiahship even as there was a problem in their recognition of the presence of the Kingdom of God.

We have discovered that the popular expectation of the coming of the Kingdom of God meant that the end of the Age and the manifestation of God's rule in power and glory, when all evil would be purged from the earth. However, Jesus taught that the Kingdom had come but in a new and unexpected form. Although the old Age goes on, the Kingdom of God has invaded the realm of Satan to deliver men from his rule. This was the mystery, the new disclosure of the divine purpose in the mission of our Lord.

This same problem was involved in the disclosure of our Lord's Messiahship. To the Jews, including the disciples of Jesus, Messiah was expected to be either a conquering Davidic King before whom the enemies of God and of God's people could not stand; or He would be a heavenly supernatural being who would come to earth with power and great glory to destroy the wicked and to bring the Kingdom of God in power (see Daniel 7). In either case, the coming of Messiah would mean the end of This Age and the appearance of the Kingdom in power.

Then Jesus appeared neither as a conquering Davidic King nor as a heavenly glorious Son of Man, but as a man among men in humility and weakness. The people could not understand how He could be their Messiah even though He performed wonderful works. At one point, they thought He might indeed be Messiah, and they tried to force His hand. After the feeding of the five thousand, when he had taken a few fish and loaves and multiplied them so as to feed a host of people, they came to take Him by force and make Him King (John 6: 15).

Such, however, was not our Lord's mission. His mission, as well as His Messiahship, was a "mystery"; it was not to bring the evil Age to its end and inaugurate The Age to Come. It was rather to bring the powers of the future Age to men in the midst of the present evil Age; and this mission involved His death. Therefore when the crowds tried to make Him king, He withdrew. This was a turning point in His ministry; and after this, "many of his disciples drew back and no longer went about with him" (John 6: 66). He was not the Messiah for whom they were looking. He said that they must eat His flesh and drink His blood (John 6: 53). What did this mean? They could not understand His words about His flesh which He would give for the life of the world (John 6: 51). The fact is, the Jews of our Lord's day did not understand the fifty-third chapter of Isaiah. They did not know that it had reference to Messiah. They were looking only for a conquering King or a heavenly Son of Man, not a Suffering Servant. Therefore they turned back and refused to follow Him. Even as they rejected His offer of the Kingdom because it was not what they were looking for, so they rejected His Messiahship because He was not the conquering, ruling monarch they desired.

Finally, however, the inner circle of the disciples began to realize that in spite of the fact that the Kingdom was not present in mighty power, in spite of the fact that Jesus was not to be a Davidic King, He was nevertheless the Messiah and the Kingdom was indeed present in His person and mission. This is the significance of Peter's confession at Caesarea Philippi. Jesus perceived that they had come to a crucial point of basic understanding, and He asked the disciples who He was. Peter finally spoke for the others: "You are the Christ, the Son of the living God" (Matt. 16:16). We do not often realize how great an achievement this represented or how difficult it was for Peter and the others to recognize Jesus' Messiahship because it was so utterly different from anything they had expected. It was indeed a realization which could come to men only through divine revelation itself (v. 17).

Once they had realized that He was the Messiah, even though in a new and unexpected role, Jesus instructed them as to His further purpose. His purpose was not that of a national restoration of Israel. On the contrary, He would create a new people. "And I tell you, you are Peter, and on this rock I will build my church, and the powers of death shall not prevail against it. I will give you the keys of the kingdom of heaven, and whatever you bind on earth shall be bound in heaven, and whatever you loose on earth shall be loosed in heaven" (Matt. 16: 18–19).

The meaning of the "rock" on which Jesus was to build His Church has been vigorously debated, although for our present purpose the answer to this question is not essential. Whether the rock is Peter's faith in the Messiahship and deity of Christ (Calvin), whether it is the person of Christ itself (Luther), or whether there is in reality an *unofficial* sense in which Peter, as the spokesman for the other disciples and the leader of the apostles and of the early Church in its first years, may be said to be the foundation on which the initial levels of the Church were erected, the result is ultimately the same. There is no evidence in the New Testament that an official authority was given to Peter which he could pass on to others. However, the Church is in fact "built upon the foundation of the apostles and prophets, Christ Jesus himself being the chief corner-stone" (Eph. 2: 20); and it is possible that our Lord addressed Peter as the representative of the apostles on whom the Church was to be erected.

In any case, our Lord indicates His purpose to build *His* Church. The particular form of this phrase is important. The Greek word, *ekklesia*, is the word most commonly used in the Greek Old Testament to refer to Israel as the people of God. The very use of this word suggests that our Lord purposed to bring into existence a new people who would take the place of the old Israel who rejected both His claim to Messiahship and His offer of the Kingdom of God. The fulfilment of this promise began at Pentecost when the Holy Spirit was poured out baptizing those who were followers of Jesus into the body of Christ and thus historically giving birth to the Church (I Cor. 12: 13).

Our present concern is to ask about the relationship between the Kingdom of God and the Church. Jesus promised to give to Peter, as the representative of the apostles and the Church, the keys of the Kingdom of Heaven. We have discovered earlier that the Kingdom of God means first of all the redemptive activity and rule of God working among men; and it is secondly the realm in which men experience the blessings of His rule. In this verse, the Kingdom of Heaven is seen as the final realm in which the blessings of God's rule are enjoyed, the realm of The Age to

Come, when every authority and power will be abolished. It is, in fact, that which is popularly thought of as "heaven". The keys of the future Kingdom of Heaven, *i.e.,* the power to open or close the doors into the blessings of The Age to Come are to be entrusted to the apostles of the Church which our Lord is to bring into being. No longer is the Kingdom of God active in the world through Israel; it works rather through the Church.

This understanding is borne out by a saying of our Lord in Luke 11: 52. Jesus condemned the Scribes because they had "taken away the key of knowledge; you did not enter yourselves, and you hindered those who were entering." The key of knowledge which should open the door of the Kingdom of God had been entrusted to the leaders of the Jewish people. This key was the correct understanding and interpretation of the Old Testament which should have led the Jews to recognize in our Lord's person and ministry the presence of the Kingdom of God and the fulfilment of the Old Testament promises. Paul expressed the same truth when he said that God had entrusted to Israel the oracles of God (Rom. 3: 2). However, the scribes had taken away the key of knowledge; they so interpreted the Scriptures that they pointed away from Christ rather than to Him as the One who had come to fulfil the prophets. Thus they refused to enter into the realm of Kingdom blessings which Jesus brought, and they hindered those who wanted to enter.

On another occasion, Jesus said to these religious leaders, "The tax collectors and the harlots go into the kingdom of God before you" (Matt. 21: 31). Of course He did not mean to say that they were really entering the blessings of the Kingdom; they were in fact standing aside and watching the publicans and harlots enter and were even trying to prevent them from entering.

This key of knowledge which in the Old Testament dispensation had been entrusted to Israel is now entrusted by our Lord to the apostles and to the Church. This fact is clearly taught in the parable of the wicked tenants in Matthew 21: 33–42. God had entrusted His vineyard to Israel. He sent to them from time to time His servants, the prophets, for an accounting, but "the tenants took his servants and beat one, killed another, and stoned another." Finally, He sent His Son thinking that they would reverence and acknowledge Him. But "they took him and cast

H

him out of the vineyard, and killed him." Jesus Himself interprets this parable in no uncertain terms: "Therefore I tell you, the kingdom of God will be taken away from you and given to a nation producing the fruits of it" (v. 43).

Here is an unambiguous statement. Israel had been the possessors of the Kingdom of God. This means that until the time of the coming of Christ in the flesh, God's redemptive activity in history had been channelled through the nation Israel and the blessings of the divine rule had been bestowed upon this people. The children of Israel were indeed the sons of the Kingdom. Gentiles could share these blessings only by entering into relationship with Israel. However, when the time came that God manifested His redemptive activity in a new and wonderful way and the Kingdom of God visited men in the person of God's Son bringing to them a fuller measure of the blessings of the divine rule, Israel rejected both the Kingdom and the Bearer of the Kingdom. Therefore, the Kingdom in its new manifestation was taken away from Israel and given to a new people.

This new people is the Church. "On this rock I will build my church." In this saying, the word "church" does not yet have the technical meaning which it acquires after Pentecost. As we have already indicated, the word means the people of God. This new people is "a chosen race, a royal priesthood, a holy nation" spoken of by Peter (I Pet. 2: 9). The Kingdom of God does not now belong to the race of Abraham but to "an elect race," for "it is men of faith who are the sons of Abraham" (Gal. 3: 7). It is not the possession of an Israelitic priesthood, for Christ has made those who constitute His Church to be "priests to his God and Father" (Rev. 1: 6). God is not now dealing with a nation after the flesh, but with a holy nation, the Church, on the basis of personal saving faith in Jesus the Son of God.

The relationship between the Church and the Kingdom of God must be clearly established. The Kingdom of God is first of all the divine redemptive rule manifested in Christ, and it is secondly the realm of sphere in which the blessings of the divine rule may be experienced. These distinctions have been carefully developed in an earlier chapter. As the divine redemptive rule of God, the Kingdom of God has come among men to defeat Satan and to deliver men from the domination of satanic power (Matt. 12: 28). Because it is a present realm in which these blessings are enjoyed, men may now enter into the Kingdom of God. The era of the law and the prophets ended with John the Baptist; from that time the Kingdom of God was preached and all who received the announcement entered vigorously, indeed "violently," into the Kingdom (Luke 16: 16). All who have received this good news of redemption have been "delivered . . . from the dominion of darkness (see II Cor. 4: 4) and transferred . . . to the kingdom of his beloved Son" (Col. 1: 13).

The Kingdom of God is at the same time the Kingdom of Christ (Eph. 5: 5); for the Kingdom of God, the redemptive reign of God, is manifested among men through the person of Christ, and it is Christ who must reign until He has put all His enemies under His feet (I Cor. 15: 25). Indeed, if any distinction is to be made between the Kingdom of God and of Christ, we must say that the Kingdom of Christ includes the period from His coming in the flesh until the end of His millennial reign "when he delivers the kingdom to God the Father" (I Cor. 15: 24).[1]

The Kingdom of God, as the redemptive activity and rule of God in Christ, created the Church and works through the Church in the world. As the disciples of the Lord went throughout the villages of Palestine, they proclaimed that in their mission, the Kingdom of God had come near to these villages (Luke 10: 9). They performed the signs of the Kingdom, healing the sick and casting out demons, thus delivering men from the satanic power (vv. 9, 17). Any city which rejected them thereby rejected the Kingdom of God and reserved for itself a fearful judgment, for in the mission of the disciples, "the kingdom of God has come near" (v. 11). Thus the Kingdom of God was at work among men not only in the person of our Lord but also through His disciples as they brought the word and the signs of the Kingdom to the cities of Galilee.

In the same way, the Kingdom of God, the redemptive activity and power of God, is working in the world today through the Church of Jesus Christ. The Church is the fellowship of disciples of Jesus who have received the life of the Kingdom and are

[1] Professor Oscar Cullmann suggests that such a distinction should be made. See above, p. 28.

dedicated to the task of preaching the Gospel of the Kingdom in the world. Philip went to Samaria preaching "good news about the kingdom of God and the name of Jesus Christ" (Acts 8: 12). Paul went to Rome and preached first to the Jews, then to the Gentiles, the Kingdom of God (Acts 28: 23, 31).

As the emissaries of our Lord went throughout the Roman world with the proclamation of the Kingdom and as today the disciples of Jesus go throughout the world with the good news about the Kingdom of God, two things always happen: some men are loosed while others are bound. Some believe and receive the message. They are delivered out of the power of darkness and transferred into the Kingdom of the Son of God's love (Col. 1: 13); that is, they enter into the Kingdom of God because they receive its blessings. Furthermore, they are assured of an entrance into the future Kingdom of God when Christ comes in glory.

Others, however, reject the good news of the Kingdom. To them, the doors of the Kingdom of God, both in the present and in the future, are closed. Christ has indeed given to His disciples, to the Church, the keys of the Kingdom of Heaven; and what His disciples bind on earth as they preach the Gospel of the Kingdom will be bound in heaven; and what they loose on earth, *i.e.,* those whom they loose from their sins, will be loosed in heaven. In a real sense of the word, it is the Church—the disciples of the Lord—who use the keys and perform the function of binding and loosing; but in a deeper sense, it is the working of the Kingdom of God through the Church which accomplishes these eternal ends. The important fact is this: The Kingdom of God does not function in a vacuum but is entrusted to men and works through redeemed men who have given themselves to the rule of God through Christ. It is, however, a dynamic and not an official function which the Church exercises.

There are a very few verses in the New Testament which equate the Kingdom with the Church, but these very verses support our conclusions. Revelation 5: 9–10 reads, "Thou wast slain and by thy blood didst ransom men for God from every tribe and tongue and people and nation, and hast made them to be a kingdom and priests to our God, and they shall reign on earth."[1] This song

[1] The present tense of the King James Version represents an inferior Greek text.

of the twenty-four elders identifies all of the redeemed as a Kingdom. Do we not therefore have the Scriptural precedent to identify the Church with the Kingdom of God? Only in this sense: the redeemed are a kingdom *because they shall reign upon the earth*. They are not a kingdom because the members of the Church are the people over whom Christ exercises His reign. They are not a kingdom because the Church is the sphere or realm in which the blessings of the redemptive reign are to be experienced. The Church is a kingdom because it shares Christ's rule. The Kingdom of God in this verse is not the realm of God's reign; it is God's reign itself, a reign which is shared with those who surrender themselves to it.

Revelation 1: 6 is to be interpreted in light of this verse. The Church is both a priesthood and a kingdom. The redeemed share the prerogative of their Great High Priest of entering into the very Holy of Holies and worshipping God. They are priests. The Church also shares the prerogative of their Lord and King. They are granted the right to rule with Christ. They are a kingdom, a nation of kings.

The Church therefore is not the Kingdom of God; God's Kingdom creates the Church and works in the world through the Church. Men cannot therefore build the Kingdom of God, but they can preach it and proclaim it; they can receive it or reject it. The Kingdom of God which in the Old Testament dispensation was manifested in Israel is now working in the world through the Church.

There is therefore but one people of God. This is not to say that the Old Testament saints belonged to the Church and that we must speak of the Church in the Old Testament. Acts 7: 28 does indeed speak of the "church in the wilderness"; but the word here does not bear its New Testament connotation but designates only the "congregation" in the wilderness. The Church properly speaking had its birthday on the day of Pentecost, for the Church is composed of all of those who by one Spirit have been baptized into one body (I Cor. 12: 13), and this baptizing work of the Spirit began on the day of Pentecost.

While we must therefore speak of Israel and the Church, we must speak of only one people of God. This is vividly clear in

Paul's illustration of the olive tree in Romans 11. There is one olive tree; it is the people of God. In the Old Testament era, the branches of the tree were Israel. However, because of unbelief, some of the natural branches were broken off and no longer belong to the tree (v. 16). We know from verse 5 that not all of the branches were broken off, for "there is a remnant, chosen by grace." Some Jews accepted the Messiah and His message of the Gospel of the Kingdom. We must remember that the earliest Church consisted of Jewish believers; but they came into the Church not because they were Jews but because they were believers.

When these natural branches were broken off, other branches were taken from a wild olive and contrary to nature grafted into the olive tree (vv. 17, 24). This refers to the Gentiles who received the Gospel of the Kingdom, the "other nation" (Matt. 21: 43) of which our Lord spoke. The natural branches which were broken off were cast from the tree because of unbelief; and the wild branches were grafted on because of their faith (v. 20). This entire procedure is "contrary to nature"; *i.e.,* it is not what one would expect from reading the Old Testament. From the Old Testament point of view, one would never know that the people of God was to consist largely of Gentiles and that the majority of the Jewish nation were to be broken off. This mixed character of the Church is indeed another mystery—a further disclosure of God's redemptive purpose which had not been revealed to the Old Testament prophets (Eph. 3: 3).

In the Old Testament era, the olive tree—the people of God— consisted of the children of Israel. Gentiles entered into the blessings of God's people only as they shared the terms of the covenant with Israel. In the New Testament dispensation, the natural branches, Israel, have been largely broken off the tree because of unbelief and wild branches from the Gentiles have been grafted in, through faith. But there is but one tree, one people of God, which consisted first of Israelites and then of believing Gentiles and Jews. It is impossible to think of two peoples of God through whom God is carrying out two different redemptive purposes without doing violence to Romans 11.

This present state of the olive tree, however, is not God's last work. Paul writes, "And even the others, if they do not persist in their unbelief, will be grafted in, for God has the power to graft them in again. . . . Lest you be wise in your own conceits, I want you to understand this mystery, brethren: a hardening has come upon part of Israel, until the full number of the Gentiles come in, and so all Israel will be saved" (Rom. 11: 23, 25 f.). The final form of the olive tree will not be one whose branches are largely wild, *i.e.,* Gentiles. Israel—the natural branches which were broken off because of unbelief—is yet to believe and be grafted again into the olive tree. Here is another "mystery," another redemptive purpose of God which was not disclosed to the prophets but which has now been revealed through the apostles. The hardening of Israel and their rejection from the people of God is only partial and temporary; it will last until the full number of the Gentiles has come in. God has a purpose to bring salvation to the Gentile peoples and He has used the unbelief of Israel to bring about the accomplishment of this redemptive purpose. But when His purpose with the wild branches has been completed, He will turn again to the natural branches; the veil will be taken away from their eyes (II Cor. 3: 16) and they will believe and be grafted again into the people of God. Thus "all Israel will be saved."

It is quite impossible in light of the context and the course of Paul's thought in this passage to understand "all Israel" to refer to the Church. There is, to be sure, a very real sense in which the Church is Israel, the sons of Abraham, the true circumcision (Gal. 3: 7; Rom. 2: 28; 4: 1, 12, 16). However, this does not mean that God has for ever cast off Israel after the flesh. Paul emphatically denies this. There is first of all a spiritual remnant—natural branches which were not broken off because they received Christ (Rom. 11: 1-6). But secondly, there is to be a greater turning to the Lord on the part of Israel after the flesh, of such proportions that Paul can say that "all Israel," *i.e.,* Israel as a whole, will be saved.

This future salvation of Israel is reflected in a few sayings of our Lord. As he was weeping over Jerusalem not long before His death, He cried, "O Jerusalem, Jerusalem, killing the prophets and stoning those who are sent to you! How often would I have gathered your children together as a hen gathers her brood under her wings, and you would not! Behold, your house is forsaken

and desolate. For I tell you, you will not see me again, until you
say, 'Blessed be he who comes in the name of the Lord'" (Matt.
23: 37–39). Jerusalem, symbolic of Israel, had rejected the
prophets whom God had sent, until finally, God sent His Son.
Jesus longed to gather Israel into the blessings of God's Kingdom
but Israel would not hear; the Son was rejected. Therefore
judgment rests upon Israel and the Holy City is to be destroyed.
The judgments of God's Kingdom have often been manifested in
history. However, this desolation of Jerusalem which was
historically accomplished in A.D. 70 when the temple was destroyed and the city ravaged by the Romans is not to be the final
word. It will be the last visitation of God to Israel until that day
comes when Israel will recognize Christ as her Messiah and will
say, "Blessed is he who comes in the name of the Lord." Israel is
yet to be saved.

Again, in Luke's account of the Olivet Discourse which fore-
cast both the historical destruction of Jerusalem and the end of the
age, we read that Jesus said of the Holy City, "Jerusalem will be
trodden down by the Gentiles, until the times of the Gentiles are
fulfilled" (Luke 21: 24). The divine judgment is to rest upon
Jerusalem and upon the Jewish nation until the "times of the
Gentiles," i.e., the divine visitation of the Gentiles is accomplished. When God's purpose for the Gentiles is fulfilled, so
this verse implies, Jerusalem will no longer be trodden down.
There will be a restoration of Israel; "all Israel will be
saved."

It is impossible in this study to enter into the question of how
this restoration and the regrafting of Israel into the people of
God is to be accomplished. The New Testament has very little to
say about the way in which God will effect this end. One fact,
however, is very important: so far as the New Testament is concerned, the salvation of Israel is an essential part of God's single
redemptive purpose. The work of God's Spirit in the formation
of the Church and the future divine visitation of Israel by which
the natural branches are regrafted into the olive tree ought not to
be seen as two separate and unrelated purposes but as two stages
of the single redemptive purpose of God through His Kingdom.
There is a single olive tree, and there is one Kingdom of God.
The final stages of the reign of God in Christ by which He will

put all His enemies under His feet (I Cor. 15: 25) will include the salvation of Israel after the flesh. The people of God through whom the Kingdom of God is working in This Age is the Church which consists largely of Gentiles; but the people of God in whom the Kingdom will come to its consummation will include Israel (Rom. 11: 12). But there is one Kingdom and there is one people.

Too often in our study of the relationship between the Kingdom of God, The Church and Israel, we lose sight of the fact which is for us of primary importance: the Kingdom of God which will finally bring salvation to Israel and which will bring Israel into the Kingdom has brought salvation to us who constitute the Church and has brought us into God's Kingdom. The Kingdom of God is working in the world through the disciples of Jesus Christ who have surrendered to the demand of the Kingdom and constitute the new people of God, the Church. The Kingdom of God has invaded the realm of Satan in the person and mission of Christ to deliver men from the bondage of darkness; and the conflict between the Kingdom of God and the powers of darkness continues as the Church bears the good news of God's Kingdom to the nations of the earth.

While the Kingdom of God will not be realized as a state of perfect blessedness until Christ returns, God's Kingdom is at work in the world and is engaged in a mortal struggle with evil. The Church is the instrument of this struggle. Conflict therefore must ever be an essential element in the life of the Church so long as This Age lasts. Human history will realize something of the life and blessings of God's Kingdom because a new community has been formed in human society. The Church is the community of the Kingdom of God and is to press the struggle against satanic evil in the world. The sons of the Kingdom cannot help but exercise an influence in human history for they are the light of the world and the salt of the earth (Matt. 5: 13–16). So long as light is light, it must shine; and so long as salt is salt, it must preserve. Thus the mission of the Church is not only that of employing the keys of the Kingdom to open to both Jew and Gentile the door into the eternal life which is the gift of God's Kingdom; it is also the instrument of God's dynamic rule in the world to oppose evil and the powers of Satan in every form of their manifestation.

When God's people lose sight of this fact, we betray our character as the Church. We are the focus of a conflict between the Kingdom of God and satanic evil. This is essentially a conflict in the spiritual realm. But these spiritual forces of satanic evil and of God's Kingdom manifest themselves in the areas of human conduct and relationships. Therefore we must press the battle against the powers of darkness wherever we find them until the day dawns and the light of the knowledge of God shall fill the earth.

CHAPTER IX

WHEN WILL THE KINGDOM COME?

FOR this final study, we shall turn to a single verse in our Lord's teachings. The truth embodied in this verse is from one point of view the most important of this entire series of studies for the Church today. It is a text whose meaning can be grasped only against the background of the larger study of the Kingdom of God.

We have discovered that the Kingdom of God is God's reign defeating His enemies, bringing men into the enjoyment of the blessings of the divine reign. We have found that God's reign is accomplished in three great acts so that we might say that the Kingdom comes in three stages. The third and final victory occurs at the end of the Millennium when death, Satan, sin are finally destroyed and the Kingdom is realized in its ultimate perfection. A second victory occurs at the beginning of the Millennium when Satan is to be chained in the bottomless pit. Apparently, however, sin and death continue throughout this period, for death is not cast into the lake of fire until the end of the Millennium.

An initial manifestation of God's Kingdom is found in the mission of our Lord on earth. Before The Age to Come, before the millennial reign of Christ, the Kingdom of God has entered into This present evil Age here and now in the person and work of Christ. We may therefore now experience its power; we may know its life; we may enter into a participation of its blessings. If we have entered into the enjoyment of the blessings of God's Kingdom, our final question is, What are we to do as a result of these blessings? Are we passively to enjoy the life of the Kingdom while waiting for the consummation at the return of the Lord? Yes, we are to wait, but not passively. Perhaps the most important single verse in the Word of God for God's people today is the text for this study: Matthew 24: 14.

This verse suggests the subject of this chapter, "When will the

Kingdom come?" This of course refers to the manifestation of God's Kingdom in power and glory when the Lord Jesus returns. There is wide interest among God's people as to the time of Christ's return. Will it be soon, or late? Many prophetic Bible conferences offer messages which search the Bible and scan the newspapers to understand the prophecies and the signs of the times to try to determine how near to the end we may be. Our text is the clearest statement in God's Word about the time of our Lord's coming. There is no verse which speaks as concisely and distinctly as this verse about the time when the Kingdom will come.

The chapter is introduced by questions of the disciples to the Lord as they looked at the Temple whose destruction Jesus had just announced. "Tell us, when will this be and what shall be the sign of your coming, and of the close of the age?" (Matt. 24: 3). The disciples expected This Age to end with the return of Christ in glory. The Kingdom will come with the inauguration of The Age to Come. Here is their question: "When will This Age end? When will you come again and bring the Kingdom?"

Jesus answered their question in some detail. He described first of all the course of This Age down to the time of the end.[1] This evil Age is to last until His return. It will for ever be hostile to the Gospel and to God's people. Evil will prevail. Subtle, deceitful influences will seek to turn men away from Christ. False religious, deceptive messiahs will lead many astray. Wars will continue; there will be famines and earthquakes. Persecution and martyrdom will plague the Church. Believers will suffer hatred so long as This Age lasts. Men will stumble and deliver up one another. False prophets will arise, iniquity abound, the love of many will grow cold.

This is a dark picture, but this is what is to be expected of an age under the world-rulers of this darkness (Eph. 6: 12). However, the picture is not one of unrelieved darkness and evil. God has not abandoned This Age to darkness. Jewish apocalyptic writings of New Testament times conceived of an age completely under the control of evil. God had withdrawn from active participation

[1] The original form of the Olivet Discourse was concerned both with the fall of Jerusalem (Luke 21: 20 ff.) and with the end of The Age. This, however, involves critical problems which cannot here be discussed.

in the affairs of man; salvation belonged only to the future when God's Kingdom would come in glory. The present would witness only sorrow and suffering.

Some Christians have reflected a similar pessimistic attitude. Satan is the "god of This Age"; therefore God's people can expect nothing but evil and defeat in This Age. The Church is to become thoroughly apostate; civilization is to be utterly corrupted. Christians must fight a losing battle until Christ comes.

The Word of God does indeed teach that there will be an intensification of evil at the end of the Age, for Satan remains the god of This Age. But we must strongly emphasize that God has not abandoned This Age to the Evil One. In fact, the Kingdom of God has entered into This Evil Age; Satan has been defeated. The Kingdom of God, in Christ, has created the Church, and the Kingdom of God works in the world through the Church to accomplish the divine purposes of extending His Kingdom in the world. We are caught up in a great struggle—the conflict of the ages. God's Kingdom works in this world through the power of the Gospel. "And this gospel of the kingdom will be preached throughout the whole world, as a testimony to all nations; and then the end will come."

In this text I find three things. There is a message, there is a mission, there is a motive. The *message* is the Gospel of the Kingdom, this Good News about the Kingdom of God.

Some Bible teachers say that the Gospel of the Kingdom is not the Gospel of salvation. It is rather a gospel announcing the return of Christ which will be preached in the tribulation by a Jewish remnant after the Church is gone. We cannot deal at length with that problem, but we can discover that the Gospel of the Kingdom is the Gospel which was proclaimed by the apostles in the early Church.

We must first, however, notice a close connexion between this verse and the Great Commission. At His Ascension, the Lord commissioned His disciples, "Go therefore and make disciples of all nations, baptizing them in the name of the Father and of the Son and of the Holy Spirit, teaching them to observe all that I have commanded you; and lo, I am with you always, to the close of the age" (Matt. 28: 19–20). When one compares these verses, they speak for themselves. "What shall be the sign of your coming, and of the close of the age?" "This gospel of the kingdom will be preached throughout the whole world, as a testimony to all nations; and then the end will come." "Go therefore and make disciples of all nations, . . . and lo, I am with you always, to the close of the age." Both verses speak about the same mission: world-wide evangelization until the end of the Age. This fact ties together Matt. 28: 19 and Matt. 24: 14.

The book of Acts relates that the apostles set out upon the fulfilment of this mission. In Acts 8: 12, Philip went down to Samaria and preached the Gospel. The Revised Standard Version accurately describes his mission in these words: "he preached good news about the kingdom of God." Literally translated, the words are, "Gospeling concerning the kingdom of God." New Testament Greek has the same root for the noun, "gospel," and the verb, "to gospel" or "to preach the gospel." It is unfortunate for our understanding of this truth that we do not have the same idiom in English. Matthew 24: 14 speaks of the "gospel of the kingdom," and Acts 8: 12 speaks of "gospeling about the kingdom." This Gospel of the Kingdom must be preached in all the world. Philip went into Samaria, *gospeling* concerning the Kingdom of God, *i.e.,* preaching the Gospel of the Kingdom. We have in Acts 8: 12 the same phrase as that in Matt. 24: 14, except that we have a verb instead of the noun with the preposition "about" inserted in the phrase.

When Paul came to Rome he gathered together the Jews, for he always preached the Gospel "to the Jew first." What was his message? "When they had appointed a day for him, they came to him at his lodging in great numbers. And he expounded the matter, from morning till evening, testifying to the kingdom of God and trying to convince them about Jesus" (Acts 28: 23). The testimony about the Kingdom of God, the Gospel of the Kingdom, was the message Paul proclaimed to the Jews at Rome.

However, Paul met the same reaction as had our Lord when he appeared in Israel announcing the Kingdom of God (Matt. 4: 17). Some believed, but the majority of the Jews rejected his message. Paul then announced the divine purpose for the Gentiles in the face of Israel's unbelief. "Let it be known to you then that this salvation of God has been sent to the Gentiles; they will listen"

(Acts 28: 28). Paul preached to the Jews the Kingdom of God; they rejected it. Therefore, "this salvation of God" was then offered to the Gentiles. The fact that the Gospel of the Kingdom of God is the same as the message of salvation is further proven by the following verses. "And he lived there two whole years at his own expense, and welcomed all who came to him, preaching the kingdom of God and teaching about the Lord Jesus Christ" (vv. 30–31). The Kingdom was preached to the Jews, and when they rejected it the same Kingdom was proclaimed to the Gentiles. The Good News about the Kingdom of God was Paul's message for both Jews and Gentiles.

We now turn again to the Scriptures which most clearly and simply describes what this Gospel of the Kingdom is. We have expounded this truth in detail in Chapter Three, so we need only review the facts. In I Corinthians 15: 24–25, Paul outlines the stages of our Lord's redemptive work. He describes the victorious issue of Christ's Messianic reign with the words, "Then comes the end, when he delivers the kingdom to God the Father after destroying every rule and every authority and power. For he must reign"—He must reign as King, He must reign in His Kingdom—"until he has put all his enemies under his feet. The last enemy to be destroyed is death."

Here is the Biblical description of the meaning of the reign of Christ by which His Kingdom shall attain its end. It is the reign of God in the person of His Son, Jesus Christ, for the purpose of putting His enemies under His feet. "The last enemy to be abolished is death." The abolition of death is the mission of God's Kingdom. God's Kingdom must also destroy every other enemy, including sin and Satan; for death is the wages of sin (Rom. 6: 23) and it is Satan who has the power over death (Heb. 2: 14). Only when death, sin, and Satan are destroyed will redeemed men know the perfect blessings of God's reigr

The Gospel of the Kingdom is the announcement of Christ's conquest over death. We have discovered that while the consummation of this victory is future when death is finally cast into the lake of fire (Rev. 20: 14), Christ has nevertheless already defeated death. Speaking of God's grace, Paul says that it has now been "manifested through the appearing of our Saviour Christ Jesus, who abolished death and brought life and immortality to light through the gospel" (II Tim. 1: 10). The word here translated "abolish" does not mean to do away with, but to defeat, to break the power, to put out of action. The same Greek word is used in I Corinthians 15: 26, "The last enemy to be *destroyed* is death." This word appears also in I Corinthians 15: 24, "Then comes the end, when he delivers the kingdom to God the Father after *destroying* every rule and every authority and power."

There are therefore two stages in the destruction—the abolition —the defeat of death. Its final destruction awaits the Second Coming of Christ; but by His death and resurrection, Christ has already destroyed death. He has broken its power. Death is still an enemy, but it is a defeated enemy. We are certain of the future victory because of the victory which has already been accomplished. We have an accomplished victory to proclaim.

This is the good news about the Kingdom of God. How men need this gospel! Everywhere one goes he finds the gaping grave swallowing up the dying. Tears of loss, of separation, of final departure stain every face. Every table sooner or later has an empty chair, every fireside its vacant place. Death is the great leveller. Wealth or poverty, fame or oblivion, power or futility, success or failure, race, creed, or culture—all our human distinctions mean nothing before the ultimate irresistible sweep of the scythe of death which cuts us all down. And whether the mausoleum is a fabulous Taj Mahal, a massive pyramid, an unmarked forgotten spot of ragged grass, or the unplotted depths of the sea, one fact stands: death reigns.

Apart from the Gospel of the Kingdom, death is the mighty conqueror before whom we are all helpless. We can only beat our fists in utter futility against the unyielding and unresponding tomb. But the Good News is this: death has been defeated; our conqueror has been conquered. In the face of the power of the Kingdom of God in Christ, death was helpless. It could not hold Him, death has been defeated; life and immortality have been brought to light. An empty tomb in Jerusalem is proof of it. This is the Gospel of the Kingdom.

The enemy of God's Kingdom is Satan; Christ must rule until He has put Satan under His feet. This victory also awaits the Coming of Christ. During the Millennium, Satan is to be bound in a bottomless pit. Only at the end of the Millennium is he to be cast into the lake of fire.

But we have discovered that Christ has already defeated Satan. The victory of God's Kingdom is not only future; a great initial victory has taken place. Christ partook of flesh and blood—He became incarnate—"that through death he might destroy him who has the power of death, that is, the devil, and deliver all those who through fear of death were subject to lifelong bondage" (Heb. 2: 14–15). The word translated "destroy" is the same word found in II Tim. 1: 10; I Cor. 15: 24 and 26. Christ has nullified the power of death; he has also nullified the power of Satan. Satan still goes about like a roaring lion bringing persecution upon God's people (I Pet. 5: 8); he insinuates himself like an angel of light into religious circles (II Cor. 11: 14). But he is a defeated enemy. His power, his domination has been broken. His doom is sure. A decisive, *the* decisive, victory has been won. Christ cast out demons, delivering men from satanic bondage, proving that God's Kingdom delivers men from their enslavement to Satan. It brings them out of darkness into the saving and healing light of the Gospel. This is the Good News about the Kingdom of God. Satan is defeated, and we may be released from demonic fear and from satanic evil and know the glorious liberty of the sons of God.

Sin is an enemy of God's Kingdom. Has Christ done anything about sin, or has He merely promised a future deliverance when He brings the Kingdom in glory? We must admit that sin, like death, is abroad in the world. Every newspaper bears an eloquent testimony of the working of sin. Yet sin, like death and Satan, has been defeated. Christ has already appeared to put away sin by the sacrifice of Himself (Heb. 9: 26). The power of sin has been broken. "We know this that our old self was crucified with him so that the body of sin might be destroyed, and we might no longer be enslaved to sin" (Rom. 6: 6). Here a third time is the word "to destroy" or "abolish." Christ's reign as King has the objective of "abolishing" every enemy (I Cor. 15: 24, 26). This work is indeed future, but it is also past. What our Lord will finish at His Second Coming He has already begun by His death and resurrection. "Death" has been abolished, destroyed (II Tim. 1: 10); Satan has been destroyed (Heb. 2: 14); and in Rom. 6: 6,

I

the "body of sin" has been abolished, destroyed. The same word
of victory, of the destruction of Christ's enemies, is used three
times of this threefold victory: over Satan, over death, over sin.

Therefore, we are to be no longer in bondage to sin (Rom.
6: 6). The day of slavery to sin is past. Sin is in the world, but
its power is not the same. Men are no longer helpless before it,
for its dominion has been broken. The power of the Kingdom of
God has invaded This Age, a power which can set men free from
their bondage to sin.

The Gospel of the Kingdom is the announcement of what God
has done and will do. It is His victory over His enemies. It is
the Good News that Christ is coming again to destroy for ever
His enemies. It is a gospel of hope. It is also the Good News of what
God has already done. He has already broken the power of death,
defeated Satan, and overthrown the rule of sin. The Gospel is one
of promise but also of experience, and the promise is grounded in
experience. What Christ has done guarantees what He will do.
This is the Gospel which we must take into all the world.

In the second place, we find in Matthew 24: 14 a *mission* as well
as a message. This Gospel of the Kingdom, this Good News of
Christ's victory over God's enemies, must be preached in all
the world for a witness to all nations. This is our mission. This
verse is one of the most important in all the Word of God to
ascertain the meaning and the purpose in human history. The
meaning of history is a problem which is today confounding the
minds of thinking men. We do not need to be reminded that our
generation faces potential destruction of such total proportions
that few of us try to envisage the awful reality. In the fact of such
threatening catastrophe, men are asking as they have never asked
before, what is history all about? Why is man on this earth?
Where is he going? Is there a thread of meaning, of purpose, of
destiny, that will bring mankind to some goal? Or, to repeat a
metaphor, are we simply a group of puppets jerking about on the
stage of history, whose fate is to have the stage burn down,
destroying the human puppets with it, leaving nothing behind
but a handful of ashes and the smell of smoke? Is this to be the
destiny of human history?

In a former generation, the philosophy of progress was widely
accepted. Some thinkers charted the meaning of history by a

single straight line which traced a gradual but steady incline from primitive savage beginnings upward to a high level of culture and civilization. The philosophy of progress taught that mankind, because of its intrinsic character, is destined to improve until it one day attains a perfect society, free from all evil, war, poverty, and conflict. This view has been shattered upon the anvil of history. Current events have made the concept of inevitable progress intolerable and unrealistic.

Another view interprets history as a series of cycles like a great spiral. There is movement both up and down. There are high points and low points on the spiral. But each ascent is a little higher than the last and each descent is not as low as the preceding. Even though we have our "ups and downs," the movement of the spiral as a whole is upward. This is a modification of the doctrine of progress.

Other interpretations have been utterly pessimistic. Someone has suggested that the most accurate chart of the meaning of history is the set of tracks made by a drunken fly with feet wet with ink, staggering across a piece of white paper. They lead nowhere and reflect no pattern of meaning. One of the greatest contemporary New Testament scholars, Rudolf Bultmann, has written, "Today we cannot claim to know the end and the goal of history. Therefore the question of meaning in history has become meaningless" (*History and Eschatology*, p. 120).

Many of the best minds of our generation are wrestling with this problem. The economic determinism of the Marxist system rests upon a philosophy of history which is materialistically grounded; but it *is* a philosophy of history and promises its adherents a destiny. Spengler believed that progress was impossible and that history was doomed to inevitable decline and degeneration. Toynbee has produced a massive study which attempts to find patterns and cycles of meaning in the history of civilizations.

On the other hand, such scholars as Niebuhr, Rust, and Piper have written learned studies which seek for the clue to the meaning of history in the Biblical truth of revelation. This is indeed a profound problem, and we do not wish to brush aside the complexities of the matter with a wave of the hand. However, it is the author's conviction that the ultimate meaning of history must be found in the action of God in history as recorded and interpreted in inspired Scripture. Here, Christian faith must speak. If there is no God, man is lost in a labyrinthine maze of bewildering experiences with no thread of meaning to guide him. If God has not acted in history, the ebb and flow of the tides of the centuries wash back and forth aimlessly between the sands of eternity. But the basic fact in the Word of God is that God has spoken, God has been redemptively at work in history; and the divine action will yet bring history to a divinely destined goal.

If there is no God who has His hand on the helm of history, I am a pessimist. But I believe in God. I believe God has a purpose. I believe God has revealed His purpose in history, in Christ and in His Word. What is that purpose? Where are its outlines to be traced?

One travels throughout the Near East and gazes with wonder upon the ruins which bear silent witness to once mighty civilizations. Massive columns still reach to the heavens, while elsewhere only huge mounds scar barren plains marking the accumulated debris of dead civilizations. The Sphinx and the pyramids of Gizeh, the pillars of Persepolis, the towers of Thebes, still bear eloquent testimony to the glory that was Egypt and Persia. One may still climb the Acropolis in Athens or tread the Forum in Rome and feel something of the splendour and glory of first-century civilizations which in some respects have never been surpassed. But today—ruins, toppled pillars, prostrate statues, dead civilizations.

What is the meaning of it all? Why do nations rise and fall? Is there any purpose? Or will the earth some day become a dead star, lifeless as the moon?

The Bible has an answer. The central theme of the entire Bible is God's redemptive work in history. Long ago, God chose a small, despised people, Israel. God was not interested in this people for their own sake; God's purpose included all mankind. God in His sovereign design selected this one insignificant people that through them He might work out His redemptive purpose which eventually would include the entire race. The ultimate meaning of Egypt, of the Assyrians, of the Chaldeans and of the other nations of the ancient Near East is found in their relationship to this one tiny nation—Israel. God set up rulers and cast them down that He might bring forth Israel. He raised up this people and preserved them. He had a plan, and He was working out this plan in history. We speak of this as Redemptive History. The Bible alone, of all ancient literatures, contains a philosophy of history, and it is a philosophy of redemption.

Then came the day when "in the fulness of time" appeared on earth the Lord Jesus Christ, a Jew, a son of Abraham after the flesh. God's purpose with Israel was then brought to a great fulfilment. This does not mean that God is done with Israel. But it does mean that when Christ appeared, God's redemptive purpose through Israel attained its initial objective. Up until that time, the clue to the meaning of the divine purpose in history was identified with Israel as a nation. When Christ had accomplished His redemptive work of death and resurrection, the divine purpose in history moved from Israel, who rejected the Gospel, to the Church—the fellowship of both Jews and Gentiles who accepted the Gospel. This is proven by our Lord's saying in Matthew 21: 43 which is addressed to the nation Israel: "The kingdom of God will be taken away from you and given to a nation producing the fruits of it." The Church is "a chosen race, a royal priesthood, a holy nation" (I Peter 2: 9); and it is in the present mission of the Church, as it carries the Good News of the Kingdom of God unto all the world, that the redemptive purpose of God in history is being worked out.

The ultimate meaning of history between the Ascension of our Lord and His return in glory is found in the extension and working of the Gospel in the world. "This gospel of the kingdom will be preached throughout the whole world, as a testimony to all nations; and then the end will come." The divine purpose in the nineteen hundred years since our Lord lived on earth is found in the history of the Gospel of the Kingdom. The thread of meaning is woven into the missionary programme of the Church. Some day when we go into the archives of heaven to find a book which expounds the meaning of human history as God sees it, we will not draw out a book depicting "The History of the West" or "The Progress of Civilization" or "The Glory of the British Empire" or "The Growth and Expansion of America." That book will be entitled, *The Preparation for and the Extension of the*

Gospel among the Nations. For only here is God's *redemptive* purpose carried forward.

This is a staggering fact. God has entrusted to people like us, redeemed sinners, the responsibility of carrying out the divine purpose in history. Why has God done it in this way? Is He not taking a great risk that His purpose will fail of accomplishment? It is now over nineteen hundred years, and the goal is not yet achieved. Why did God not do it Himself? Why did He not send hosts of angels whom He could trust to complete the task at once? Why has He committed it to us? We do not try to answer the question, except to say that such is God's will. Here are the facts: God has entrusted to us this mission; and unless we do it, it will not get done.

This is also a thrilling fact. The Christian Church today often has an inferiority complex. A few generations ago the pastor of a church was the most educated and respected leader in the community. There was a day when, because of this cultural situation, the Church exercised the predominant influence in the structure of Western community life. That day has long passed. We have often felt that the world has thrust the Church into a corner and passed us by. The Church does not count in the world at large. The United Nations is not calling upon the Church for advice in the solution of its problems. Our political leaders do not often depend upon leaders in the Church for their guidance. Science, industry, labour, education: these are the circles where wisdom and leadership are usually sought. The Church is brushed aside. Sometimes we get that feeling that we really do not count. We are on the margin of influence, we have been pushed over on to the periphery instead of standing squarely in the centre; and we pity ourselves and long for the world to pay attention to us. Thus we fall into a defensive attitude and attempt to justify our existence. Indeed, our main concern seems often to be that of self-preservation, and we assume a defeatist interpretation of our significance and of our role in the world!

Let this verse burn in our hearts. God has said this about no other group of people. This Good News of the Kingdom of God must be preached, if you please, by the Church in all the world for a witness to all nations. This is *God's* programme. This means that for the ultimate meaning of modern civilization and the destiny of human history, you and I are more important than the United Nations. What the Church does with the Gospel has greater significance ultimately than the decisions of the Kremlin. From the perspective of eternity, the mission of the Church is more important than the march of armies or the actions of the world's capitals, because it is in the accomplishment of this mission that the divine purpose for human history is accomplished. No less than this is our mission.

Let us be done with this inferiority complex. Let us for ever lay aside this attitude of self-pity and lamentation over our insignificance. Let us recognize what we are as God sees us and let us be about our divinely appointed programme. This Good News about the Kingdom must be preached in all the world for a witness to all nations and then shall the end come. I am glad, indeed proud, to be a part of the Church of Christ because to us has been committed the most meaningful and worthwhile task of any human institution. This gives to my life an eternal significance, for I am sharing in God's plan for the ages. The meaning and destiny of history rests in my hands.

Finally, our text contains a mighty *motive*. "Then the end will come." The subject of this chapter is, When will the Kingdom come? I am not setting any dates. I do not know when the end will come. And yet I do know this: When the Church has finished its task of evangelizing the world, Christ will come again. The Word of God says it. Why did He not come in A.D. 500? Because the Church had not evangelized the world. Why did He not return in A.D. 1000? Because the Church had not finished its task of world-wide evangelization. Is He coming soon? He is— if we, God's people, are obedient to the command of the Lord to take the Gospel into all the world.

What a sobering realization this is! It is so staggering that some people say, "I cannot believe it! It simply cannot be true that God has committed such responsibility to men." When William Carey wanted to go to India to take the Gospel to that country a century and a half ago, he was told, "Sit down, young man; when God wants to evangelize the heathen, He will do it without your help." But Carey had the vision and the knowledge of God's Word not to sit down. He rose up and went to India. He initiated the modern day of world-wide missions.

God has entrusted to us the continuation and the consummation of that task. Here is the thing that thrills me. We have come far closer to the finishing of this mission than any previous generation. We have done more in the last century and a half in world-wide evangelization then all the preceding centuries since the apostolic age. Our modern technology has provided printing, automobiles, aeroplanes, radios, and many other methods of expediting our task of carrying the Gospel into all the world. Previously unknown languages are being reduced to writing. The Word of God has now been rendered, in part at least, into over 1,100 languages or dialects, and the number is growing yearly. Here is the challenging fact. If God's people in the English-speaking world alone took this text seriously and responded to its challenge, we could finish the task of world-wide evangelization in our own generation and witness the Lord's return.

Someone will say, "This is impossible. Many lands today are not open to the Gospel. We cannot get into China; the doors into India are closing. If the Lord's Return awaits the evangelization of the world by the Church, then Christ cannot possibly return in our lifetime, for so many lands are today closed to the Gospel that it is impossible to finish the task today."

Such an attitude fails to reckon with God. It is true that many doors are closed at the moment; but God is able to open closed doors overnight, and God is able to work behind closed doors. Remember Abyssinia! My concern is not with closed doors; my concern is with the doors that are open which we do not enter. If God's people were really faithful and were doing everything possible to finish the task, God would see to it that the doors were opened. Our responsibility is the many doors standing wide open which we are not entering. We are a disobedient people. We argue about the definition of world-wide evangelization and we debate the details of eschatology, while we neglect the command of the Word of God to evangelize the world.

Someone else will say, "How are we to know when the mission is completed? How close are we to the accomplishment of the task? Which countries have been evangelized and which have not? How close are we to the end? Does this not lead to date-setting?"

I answer, I do not know. God alone knows the definition of terms. I cannot precisely define who "all the nations" are. Only God knows exactly the meaning of "evangelize." He alone, who has told us that this Gospel of the Kingdom shall be preached in the whole world for a testimony unto all the nations, will know when that objective has been accomplished. But I do not need to know. I know only one thing: Christ has not yet returned; therefore the task is not yet done. When it is done, Christ will come. Our responsibility is not to insist on defining the terms of our task; our responsibility is to complete it. So long as Christ does not return, our work is undone. Let us get busy and complete our mission.

Our responsibility is not to save the world. We are not required to transform This Age. The very paragraph of which this verse is the conclusion tells us that there will be wars and troubles, persecutions and martyrdoms until the very end. I am glad these words are in the Bible. They give me stability. They provide sanity. They keep me from an unrealistic optimism. We are not to be discouraged when evil times come.

However, we have a message of power to take to the world. It is the Gospel of the Kingdom. Throughout the course of This Age, two forces are at work: the power of Evil, and the Kingdom of God. The world is the scene of a conflict. The forces of the Evil One are assaulting the people of God; but the Gospel of the Kingdom is assaulting the kingdom of Satan. This conflict will last to the end of The Age. Final victory will be achieved only by the return of Christ. There is no room for an unqualified optimism. Our Lord's Olivet Discourse indicates that until the very end, evil will characterize This Age. False prophets and false messiahs will arise and lead many astray. Iniquity, evil, are so to abound that the love of many will grow cold. God's people will be called upon to endure hardness. "In the world you have tribulation" (John 16: 33). "Through many tribulations we must enter the kingdom of God" (Acts 14: 22). We must always be ready to endure the tribulation as well as the kingdom and patience which are in Jesus (Rev. 1: 9). In fact, our Lord himself said, "He who endures to the end will be saved" (Matt. 24: 13). He who endures tribulation and persecution to the uttermost, even to the laying down of his life, will not perish but will find salvation.

"Some of you they will put to death. . . . But not a hair of your head will perish" (Luke 21: 16, 18). The Church must always in its essential character be a martyr church. As we carry the Gospel into all the world, we are not to expect unqualified success. We are to be prepared for opposition, resistance, even persecution and martyrdom. This Age remains evil, hostile to the Gospel of the Kingdom.

There is, however, no room for an unrelieved pessimism. In some prophetic studies, we receive the impression that the end of the Age, the last days, are to be characterized by *total* evil. Undue emphasis is sometimes laid upon the perilous character of the last days (II Tim. 3: 1). The visible Church, we are told, is to be *completely* leavened by evil doctrine. Apostasy is so to pervade the Church that only a small remnant will be found faithful to God's Word. The closing days of This Age will be the Laodicean period when the entire professing Church will be nauseatingly indifferent to eternal issues. In such a portrayal of the last days, God's people can expect only defeat and frustration. Evil is to reign. The Church age will end with an unparalleled victory of evil. Sometimes so much stress is laid upon the evil character of the last days that we receive the impression (unintended, to be sure) that the faster the world deteriorates the better, for the sooner the Lord will come.

It cannot be denied that the Scriptures emphasize the evil character of the last days. In fact, we have already made this emphasis. The evil which characterizes This Age will find a fearful intensification at the very end in its opposition to and hatred of the Kingdom of God. This does not mean, however, that we are to lapse into pessimism and abandon This Age and the world to evil and Satan. The fact is, the Gospel of the Kingdom is to be proclaimed throughout the world. The Kingdom of God has invaded This present evil Age. The powers of The Age to Come have attacked This Age. The last days will indeed be evil days; but "*in these last days* (God) has spoken to us by a Son" (Heb. 1: 2). God has given us a Gospel of salvation for the last days, a Gospel embodied in One who is Son of God. Furthermore, "*in the last days* it shall be," God declares, "that I will pour out my Spirit upon all flesh" (Acts 2: 17). God has spoken for the last days; God has poured out His Spirit in the last day to give power to proclaim the divine Word. The last days will be evil, but not unrelieved evil. God has given us a Gospel for the last days, and He has given a power to take that Gospel into all the world for a testimony unto all the nations: then shall the end come. This must be the spirit of our mission in This evil Age. We are not rosy optimists, expecting the Gospel to conquer the world and establish the Kingdom of God. Neither are we despairing pessimists who feel that our task is hopeless in the face of the evil of This Age. We are realists, Biblical realists, who recognize the terrible power of evil and yet who go forth in a mission of worldwide evangelization to win victories for God's Kingdom until Christ returns in glory to accomplish the last and greatest victory.

Here is the motive of our mission: the final victory awaits the completion of our task. "And then the end will come." There is no other verse in the Word of God which says, "And then the end will come." When is Christ coming again? When the Church has finished its task. When will This Age end? When the world has been evangelized. "What will be the sign of your coming and of the close of the age?" (Matt. 24: 3). "This gospel of the kingdom will be preached throughout the whole world as a testimony to all nations; and then, AND THEN, the end will come." When? Then; when the Church has fulfilled its divinely appointed mission.

Do you love the Lord's appearing? Then you will bend every effort to take the Gospel into all the world. It troubles me in the light of the clear teaching of God's Word, in the light of our Lord's explicit definition of our task in the Great Commission (Matt. 28: 18–20) that we take it so lightly. "All authority in heaven and on earth has been given to me." This is the Good News of the Kingdom. Christ has wrested authority from Satan. The Kingdom of God has attacked the kingdom of Satan; This evil Age has been assaulted by The Age to Come in the person of Christ. All authority is now His. He will not display this authority in its final glorious victory until He comes again; but the authority is now His. Satan is defeated and bound; death is conquered; sin is broken. All authority is His. "Go ye therefore." Wherefore? Because all authority, all power is His, and because He is waiting until we have finished our task. His is the Kingdom;

He reigns in heaven, and He manifests His reign on earth in and through His Church. When we have accomplished our mission, He will return and establish His Kingdom in glory. To us it is given not only to wait for but also to hasten the coming of the day of God (II Pet. 3: 12). This is the mission of the Gospel of the Kingdom, and this is our mission.

INDEX OF SUBJECTS

INDEX OF SCRIPTURE